COMIC BOOK Collecting for FUN and PROFIT

by Mike Benton

Crown Publishers, Inc.
New York

For Laura,
who reads them, too

Published by Crown Publishers, Inc., One Park Avenue, New York, New York 10016 and simultaneously in Canada by General Publishing Company Limited

Manufactured in the United States of America

CROWN is a trademark of Crown Publishers, Inc.

Library of Congress Cataloging in Publication Data

Benton, Mike.
   Comic book collecting for fun and profit.

    1. Comic books, strips, etc.—Collectors and collection.   I. Title.

PN6714.B4   1985   741.5′075   84-19979

ISBN 0-517-55702-9

Designed by J. Victor Thomas

10 9 8 7 6 5 4 3 2 1

First Edition

CONTENTS

Acknowledgments.................................... ix

1. Comic Books for Fun and Profit 1

WHO COLLECTS COMIC BOOKS? ... WHY PEOPLE COLLECT COMIC
BOOKS ... THE HISTORY OF COMIC BOOK COLLECTING ... WHAT THIS
BOOK IS ALL ABOUT

2. Comic Collecting for Beginners........................... 9

IDENTIFYING THE COMIC BOOK ... COLLECTING BY NUMBERS ...
CONDITION OF A COMIC BOOK AND ITS VALUE ... HOW TO BECOME
AN EXPERT ... THE COMIC BOOK STORE ... Learning from Other Collec-
tors ... The Comic Convention ... Collector Publications ... The Price Guide
... Other Books on Comics and Collecting ... TALKING LIKE A COLLECTOR
... A GLOSSARY OF COLLECTOR TERMS

3. The Many Ways of Comic Collecting 23

THE BEGINNING COLLECTOR ... THE OLDER COLLECTOR ... THE DIF-
FERENT METHODS OF COLLECTING ... Collecting by Title ... Collecting by
Publisher or Comic Company ... Collecting by Artist ... Collecting by Comic
Type ... Collecting by Time Period ... Collecting by Cover ... Collecting by
Numbers ... Collecting by Content ... IS THERE LIFE BEYOND COMICS? ...
Original Art ... Foreign Comics ... Newspaper Strips ... Big Little Books ...
Gum Cards

4. How to Find and Buy Comic Books........................ 34

GETTING NEW COMIC BOOKS ... Comics from the Newsstand ... New Comics by Mail ... New Comics from Comic Book Store ... FINDING OLD COMICS
... Friends and Relatives ... Your Local Community ... Other Local Collectors
... Comic Book Conventions ... Mail-Order Dealers ... Buying Old Comics
from Retail Stores ... THE ART OF BUYING COMICS ... Ready for Inspection

...Handling a Comic...Discounts and Bargaining...Overpriced Comics...
Underpriced Comics

5.   Condition, Scarcity, and Values of Comic Books..........50

THE DIFFERENT CONDITIONS OF A COMIC BOOK...LEARNING HOW
TO GRADE A COMIC...Printing Defects...Aging Defects...Wear Defects
...DAMAGED COMICS...THE STANDARD GRADING DEFINITIONS...
GRADING: A STEP-BY-STEP GUIDE...The Fair Test...The Good Test...
The Very Good Test...The Fine Test...The Very Fine Test...The Near-Mint
Test...The Mint Test...HOW CONDITION AFFECTS A COMIC'S PRICE
...CONDITION AND AVAILABILITY...ALPHABET SOUP...Condition
Abbreviations...Defect Abbreviations...PRACTICAL TIPS FOR DETER-
MINING A COMIC'S CONDITION

6.   Taking Care of Your Collection............................72

THE BEST PLACE FOR YOUR COMICS...THE WORST PLACES TO STORE
YOUR COMIC COLLECTION...WAYS TO PRESERVE YOUR COMIC
BOOKS...Plastic Bags...Mylar Bags...Deacidification...Encapsulation
and Lamination...TO BOX OR NOT TO BOX...Cardboard Sheets...RE-
PAIRING AND RESTORING COMIC BOOKS...KEEPING TRACK OF YOUR
COLLECTION...Computers and Comics...Keeping Track by Pencil and
Paper

7.   What Makes a Comic Book Valuable?....................87

POPULARITY OF THE ARTIST...The Major Artists...The Notable Artists
...The New Artists...POPULARITY OF THE CHARACTER OR COMIC
TITLE...THE HISTORICAL SIGNIFICANCE OF THE BOOK...Popularity
of the Comic Book Company...Condition of Comic Books and Their Value...
Supply and Demand

8.   Making Money: Investing in Comics......................96

BASIC FACTS (AND A DISCOURAGING WORD) ABOUT INVESTING IN
COMICS...BUYING FOR INVESTMENT...INVESTMENT-QUALITY
BOOKS...THE LONG AND SHORT OF COMIC BOOK INVESTMENT...
Comics as a Short-Term Investment (Speculation)...Long-Term Investments in
Comics...TRENDS IN COMIC BOOK COLLECTING...Looking to the Past
...Price Increases and Fluctuations...WHICH COMICS TO INVEST IN:
BUILDING YOUR PORTFOLIO...A FINAL WORD ON COMIC BOOK IN-
VESTMENTS

9.   What Are Your Comics Really Worth?....................115

APPRECIATION RATE OF COMIC BOOKS...THE SIX DIFFERENT VAL-
UES OF A COMIC BOOK...Salvage Price...Intrinsic Worth...Support
Price...Buy Price...Sell Price...Price-Guide Value

10. **Cash from Comics: Selling Your Collection** 123

ALL OR NOTHING? . . . WHEN IS THE BEST TIME TO SELL? . . . WHO WILL
BUY YOUR COMICS . . . Selling to Dealers . . . Selling to Collectors . . . THE
DIFFERENT WAYS OF SELLING COMICS . . . Selling by Mail . . . Advertising
Your Collection . . . Selling by Auction . . . Selling Comics at a Convention . . .
Selling at a Retail Store

11. **Questions About Comic Books and Collecting** 134

12. **The Future of Comic Collecting** 143

THE COMPUTERS ARE COMING! . . . THE COLLECTOR'S MARKET WILL
GROW . . . COLLECTING TRENDS

Appendix   How to Become an Expert:
Source Materials for the Collector 145

COLLECTOR AND FAN PUBLICATIONS . . . COLLECTOR'S PRICE GUIDES
. . . LIBRARY BOOKS AND OTHER REFERENCE WORKS . . . LIBRARIES
AND MUSEUMS . . . Libraries with Special Comic Collections . . . Museums
with Comic Books and Original Comic Art

ACKNOWLEDGEMENTS

My sincere thanks to Julian Bach and Peter Cannon for their faith and their help in making this book a reality.

To Sally Pomeroy and Marvel Comics, and to Dee Nelson and DC Comics, my appreciation for their cooperation.

For the photographs and drawings in the book, Scott Deschaine must take full credit. Thanks, Scott.

For permission to use selected material and for his service to comic collectors everywhere, thanks to Robert M. Overstreet.

To Don Regelin, Vaughn Ritchie, Ron Tatar, and the Austin Books World of Fantasy specialty bookstore—thanks for the photographs, advice, memories, and "good deals."

I am also indebted to the many fine writers, researchers, and journalists in the comic-collecting field, such as Robert Greenberger, Catherine Yronwode, Don and Maggie Thompson, Jerry Bails, and Michael Barrier—to mention but a few.

To the hundreds of fans, collectors, and dealers who have made this hobby so much fun (Roy Bonario, Roger Stewart, Bill Wallace, Anthony Smith, and legions of unnamed others), thanks to all of you.

And a special thanks to my mother for never, ever throwing away any of my old comic books.

COMIC BOOKS FOR FUN AND PROFIT

Comic books appeal to people in every age group and economic bracket. Last year 150 million new comics were sold nationwide. An estimated 5,000 dealerships serve nearly 30 million readers, and the ranks of collectors and investors are increasing all the time.

Since the 1930s, people have read, saved, swapped, and treasured the comics. Collections are passed from parents to children, and every day another new collector discovers the exciting world of comic books.

A comic book is like no other form of entertainment or medium in the world. It's a combination of art and literature that can be appreciated by both the very young and the very sophisticated. It's a ticket to a rich world of imagination and fantasy, a passport to other realities, and an invitation to live and relive your favorite adventures over and over.

No wonder people collect comic books.

Collecting comics is different from all other collecting activities. A collection of coins or stamps or rare glassware gives its owner some pleasure from acquiring, organizing, and displaying the items. But once you have a rare stamp or a valuable coin or an antique punch bowl, there is little more that you can do with it, other than show it off.

A comic book collection, however, is a source of far greater pleasure and interest. Not only can you have fun by simply collecting comics, you can get hours and hours of satisfaction from reading, studying, researching, and talking about them. You don't just display a comic book collection; you read it and you develop an appreciation for the different artists and writers who create the comics.

Collecting comics can not only provide you with years of pleasure, but may even pay you well for the time you spend. Collectors are often pleasantly surprised to find out that all the comics they have collected and enjoyed are now worth much more than they paid for them.

Maybe you read comic books only for the love of it, or perhaps you only want to sell them for money. Either way, this book is for you—the comic reader, collector, and investor.

Who Collects Comic Books?

Are comics just for kids? Unfortunately, most people still think so. Mention collecting comic books, and you'll usually get the response, Oh, yeah. Comic books. I used to collect them—when I was a kid.

In the general public's eye, comic book collecting has a status roughly between collecting beer cans and collecting Barbie dolls. Comic books are dismissed as junk-food literature full of flying costumed characters and talking ducks. The typical comic collector is seen as an emotionally arrested adolescent who lives in a world of fantasy.

And now here's a surprise: According to a survey in *The Comics Buyers' Guide,* the average comic collector has six more years of education than the typical American. He or she has an above-average income, is well read in several other areas, and spends more on books and literature than the typical college freshman.

The longtime comic collector is likely to be either a college student or a professional worker. Just about half of all collectors are married. Almost three-fourths of them have some college training, and over 20 percent of them have completed postgraduate university work.

The average age of a serious comic collector is about 28. He is much more likely to be male than female (by about 20 to 1).

There is a higher percentage of such professional people as doctors, lawyers, engineers, writers, and artists that read and collect comics than in the general population.

So much for facts and survey results. From an admittedly biased observation, I find most comic collectors to be above average in imagination and intelligence. They are extraordinarily literate and enjoy reading fiction and nonfiction in addition to comic books. The typical collector spends over $75 per month on books and other reading materials.

Above all else, comic collectors have an excellent sense of humor, which no doubt helps when people continually ask them, Why do you waste all your time reading funny books?

Who collects comic books? Above-average, imaginative, intelligent children, teenagers, and adults. Welcome to the club.

Why People Collect Comic Books

People read comic books for fun, relaxation, and escape. But why do they bother to *collect* them?

The obvious answer is that man himself is a collecting creature. Everybody has a collection of something. Some people collect coins, stamps, or antique glass. Others collect knickknacks, high-heel shoes, lampshades, marbles, or soft-drink bottles. Why shouldn't people collect comic books as well? Comics are especially appealing to the collecting mentality.

Each issue of a comic has a number. You can collect all the comics in order, by their number and title. And there are plenty of comics to collect —more than even the most dedicated collector can ever hope to assemble.

But beyond this obvious reason for collecting comics are deeper appeals. Comic books are first and foremost collected for the memories they evoke. Call it nostalgia or just taking a trip into yesteryear, but comic books are a link between an uncertain present and a rose-colored past.

It's no secret that the "best" comic books are always the ones you read as a kid. You remember these comics fondly because they are associated with childhood and simpler times. When you reread a comic from your past, you reconnect with those emotions and thoughts that made up your early life and formed your present being. By collecting books you read one year, five years, or thirty years ago, you preserve a part of your personal history. And you thought you were only saving comic books!

Another popular reason for collecting comic books is the enjoyment to be had from understanding and learning all about a vast literature. There are over 17,000 comic book titles, approximately a quarter-million *different* comic book issues, and millions and millions of comic book pages. If you started right now, it would be impossible to read all the comic books that have ever been published.

This makes the comic book field a ripe area for study and scholarship. Hundreds of different artists and writers have worked in the comic book industry. Collectors like to study the works of these individual creators, chronicle their careers, and develop indexes to their works.

Many collectors research, write, and discuss the characters in the comics. They also analyze and evaluate the works of the men and women who created this wealth of literature.

There is a little bit of researcher, scholar, and connoisseur in all collectors, and the comic book field is an abundantly rich area for all of these endeavors.

A comic book collection can also provide a ticket to an alternate reality. Comic book characters, much like those in the soap operas on television, have their own internal world that can be easily understood. It is satisfying to read the latest exploits of a favorite comic character and share in his growth and development.

If you have a 20-year collection of Spider-Man comics, for example, then you can become involved with the world of this character as he changes and grows through the years. You share his problems, his triumphs, and his self-discoveries. In short, collecting comics lets you enter a richly textured world of familiar characters that become your literary friends and companions.

Finally, collecting comics is often done for profit, to get a good return on money invested. So often, many hobbies take up both time and money. The cash you spend on a leisure-time pursuit is often money you'll never see again. Go to a movie, eat at a restaurant, or take a vacation, and all you'll have at the end is a pleasant memory and a smaller bank account.

If you collect comics wisely, however, you will almost assuredly get back all or most of the money you spend on the hobby. And if you are knowledgeable about how you spend your collecting dollars, you will probably get back enough extra money to repay you for all the time you spent buying and reading comics.

A comic book is both a source of pleasure and a tangible investment. It's not money wasted. Indeed, it could be money very well spent, as you'll discover later in this book.

Yet collecting comics should not be done for money alone. Stocks, bonds, precious metals, and even agricultural commodities are safer and more conventional investment avenues. The money to be made from collecting comic books is a bonus. The real payoff is the hours and hours of pleasure that such a collection provides.

And really, what other reason do you need?

The History of Comic Book Collecting

People have collected comic books even before there were comic books! The first comic collectors cut and saved comic strips from daily and Sunday newspapers during the early 1900s. These strips were pasted into albums, and *voilà,* the first "comic books" were created.

As the newspaper comic strips gained popularity, Cupples and Leon Publishing Company collected the more widely read strips of the day, such as Little Nemo, Bringing Up Father, Buster Brown, and Mutt and Jeff, into cardboard bound books. The early twentieth-century American was fascinated with this new art form, and the books with comic characters sold rapidly. Other publishers issued their own books of comic-strip reprints throughout the 1920s and 1930s, and many homes soon had the beginnings of a "comic book collection." Since these comic books were similar in appearance to regular bound books, they often became a part of the permanent home library.

By the early 1930s, several publishers of inexpensive magazines ("pulps") decided to issue their own comic-strip reprint books. These books, however, were done in a colorful magazine format instead of the cardboard-bound editions of the earlier years. Readers of the 1930s became fascinated with the new comic magazines, and people were saving the early comic books as curiosity items as early as the mid-1930s, much as the first stamp collectors did with the British postage stamps in the 1840s.

Because comic books were sold on the same newsstands as the science fiction and adventure pulp magazines, they often attracted a similar readership. Some of the earliest serious comic book collectors were also

4

people who had been collecting science-fiction pulp magazines from the 1930s.

A few of these science-fiction collectors were "completists"—that is, they wanted a copy of every book or magazine that might be related in any way to the science-fiction or fantasy field. Since the first comic books were often created by fans, writers, and artists in the science-fiction field, they became sought after and collectible as imaginative literature.

One of the first famous comic book collectors was a Tennessee minister who purchased everything even remotely related to science fiction. From 1936 to 1943, he bought a copy of every comic book that was ever published. By the mid-1940s, even he could not keep up with the hundreds of titles that were appearing monthly.

There were other collectors during the 1940s, but most of our information about them comes only from the collections they left behind to their friends and families. In the mid-1970s, one such collection was discovered in Colorado. The man had lived with his two sisters and had purchased a copy of almost every major comic title from the mid-1940s to the early 1950s. He had saved these books in perfect condition in his library. When he died, his sisters discovered his massive comic collection. They were about to throw them away until their lawyer stopped them. He later located a buyer for the fabulous collection, and hundreds of rare comics were thus preserved for the collectors of today.

Most early collections, unfortunately, did not survive. Thousands of books were lost to paper drives during the war, and more were discarded in the early 1950s as comic books came under attack by various psychiatrists and educators.

In the early 1950s, a comic book company known as EC Comics began publishing science fiction, horror, crime, and war comics that appealed to a more mature audience. The stories and artwork were exceptional, and readers soon started collecting the EC comics in earnest. Back issues were advertised and traded through the comic books' letter pages, and fan clubs were started so that members might find and buy older issues of the EC Comics line. This activity marked the first organized attempt at comic collecting. Before this time, most collectors worked alone on their hobby.

Only a few hundred collectors, at most, existed during the 1950s. These individuals often did not know about other collectors. There were no stores specializing in back-issue comic books. Only a very few magazine and rare-book dealers did any business in old comic books. Almost any comic, no matter how old or rare, could be purchased for under a dollar —if the collector was lucky enough to find it.

Then 1960 came. The year before, DC Comics had published the first issue of the new *Flash Comics* (#105), which was a continuation of a title from the 1940s. Old-time comic fans became excited about DC's attempts to revive their costumed heroes in current comic books. A few science-fiction fans started writing about these new comic books in their own fanzines. A letter column in a DC comic in February of 1961 printed the names and addresses of several comic fans and collectors. These collectors contacted each other and soon established an informal network.

In 1961, five different comic collectors' magazines appeared. Most of these magazines had circulations of under 200, but they reached enough serious fans and collectors to start an organized comic-collecting movement.

As early as 1962, these new comic fans were publishing indexes and guides to their favorite comic books. They started creating their own strips, published their own magazines with ads for back-issue comics, and even gave awards to the best comic books of the year.

In 1964, comic fans in Detroit, Chicago, and New York gathered in regional meetings and traded comics and information. These marked the first official comic book conventions. Science-fiction fans had held their first such gathering in 1939, but the comic collectors soon started making up for lost time.

By 1965, there was widespread publicity about comics and comic collecting, due to Jules Feiffer's book *The Great Comic Book Heroes* and the high prices that collectors were starting to pay for valuable back issues. (One such "high" price was $50 for the first issue of Batman Comics—a book that is now worth more than a hundred times that early price.) This was the year that the general public first realized there were comic collectors and that the hobby was indeed legitimate.

By 1966, several full-time comic book dealers were issuing comic book catalogs and lists. Fans were contacting each other through the letter pages of the comics, and conventions were held in many major cities. Comic collecting was now a major hobby.

By the beginning of the 1970s, comic collecting had come a long way. There was a regular weekly newspaper for collectors who just wanted to buy and sell comics. An official price guide had finally been released, and the first paraphernalia of the comic-collecting hobby—plastic bags for storing comics—came onto the scene.

By the mid- to late 1970s, comic collectors were starting to own and operate comic book specialty shops. At these specialized stores, collectors could buy both new and old issues of their favorite comic books, get the latest price guide, stock up on plastic bags and comic boxes to hold their collections, and talk about their favorite subject—comics—with other interested collectors.

During this same time, comic conventions were being held in every major city and every state in the country. A collector could attend a convention every weekend, if he had the time and money.

The 1980s have seen the emergence of the true collector market. Now the major comic companies are developing and printing comics just for collectors. New comic companies are being started by former fans and collectors to produce new comics specifically for the collector's market. Most of the people who draw and write comics today were the fans and collectors of the 1960s and 1970s.

Comic collecting has not only grown up—it's taken over!

What This Book Is All About

Collecting comics should always be done first for the personal pleasure and satisfaction it gives. Yet comics can also be bought, sold, and traded as investment items, just like any other collectible.

This book is a guide for those who wish to collect and read comics for fun, but it is also a handbook for the comic book investor and speculator. You'll learn how to find and buy old comic books, how to take care of them, organize them, store them, and, finally, sell them. And you'll also learn how buying and selling comics can provide you with an extra income or maybe even a full-time career.

Many comic readers and fans are interested in the financial side of comic collecting. They want to know how much their comics are worth, which comics will become valuable, and how much money they can make from investing wisely in certain comics.

And that's only natural. Why shouldn't you be able to profit from an activity that also gives you so much pleasure?

There is money in comic books. Many collectors make several hundred or several thousand extra dollars a year from buying and selling comics. Serious investors with large amounts of capital have achieved a 20-percent or greater return on their money—about twice as good as most conventional investment avenues.

And there are those few lucky collectors and speculators who have not only doubled their money on comics but have achieved such astounding returns as ten times, a hundred times, and even a thousand times their initial investments! You can't make that kind of money in many other honest ventures.

Prices for some of the outstanding comic books are indeed mind-boggling. Books that sold for $50 or $100 25 years ago now command $5,000 to $10,000. A new comic book purchased for under a dollar can be worth $25 within a year's time.

Obviously there is good money to be made from collecting and investing in comic books, and that alone is a legitimate reason to buy and save comics. Yet we all know that comic books are truly priceless. The hours of enjoyment from reading and rereading your favorite comic books through the years yield rewards that simply cannot be gauged in dollars and cents. The collector who sees comic books as only a means to wealth is a poor person indeed.

But the fact of life is that comic books do cost money, and some of the best comics may even be quite expensive. The devoted reader of comic books, the true dyed-in-the-wool fan, has mixed feelings about comic book prices, collector/investors, dealers, speculators, price guides, and all the other money-related aspects of collecting and enjoying comics.

There is a popular yet mistaken belief that if you do something for pleasure (like reading and collecting comic books) you shouldn't mix it with business (like buying, selling, and investing in comics). Yet you can still collect and read comics for fun while you also buy and sell them for profit.

Why shouldn't you make money from an activity that you also happen to enjoy immensely? In fact, what better way to make money?

And the more money you make from comic books, the more comic books you can have and collect.

There is nothing wrong with mixing fun and profit. Collecting comics should be done first for the enjoyment it gives, but never turn up your nose at a chance to use your knowledge about comics to make some extra money.

This book is about both sides of comic collecting—the "fun" side and the "money" side.

Read, enjoy, and profit.

COMIC COLLECTING FOR BEGINNERS

Let's explain the mysteries of comic collecting and get you started on the right track.

First, what's the difference between collecting comics and just reading and saving them?

A *collector* always has an organized system for buying and saving comics. He selects certain comic book titles that he wants to read and save and then tries to get as many issues of that title as he can. Besides buying the new issues of a comic title, he also searches for older issues of that title. He usually has a collecting goal, such as to get every issue published of his favorite comic character.

He keeps his comics stored carefully and in order, so that he can tell which issues he has and which ones he still needs. He spends time reading not only comic books, but also books and magazines about comics, their creators, and the history of comic books. He may visit comic book stores or comic book conventions, where he can find comics that he needs or wants to read.

A casual comic book reader, on the other hand, probably buys whatever comic is handy, reads it once or twice, then tosses it into a pile or box of unorganized books and magazines. He *accumulates* comics, but he doesn't really collect them. Collecting requires some organization and thought.

Most collectors start out by organizing the comics they already own into a collection. They do this by separating their comics into piles according to *publisher* (all the Marvels in one stack, all the DC comics in another, and so on), or by *title* (Superman here, Spider-Man there), or even by the *artist* who drew the comic. After they have their collection arranged by major categories (publisher, title, artist, etc.), then they organize the comics in some sort of alphabetical, numerical, or chronological order. All this organizing makes it easy to determine which issues may be missing and to locate any issue they may want to reread, trade, or sell.

9

Organization makes the different between a collection of comics and a pile of comics.

Identifying the Comic Book

Let's take a close look at what you're collecting—the comic book itself.

To a collector, one of the most important things is being able to identify a comic book properly. A comic book is identified in several ways:

1. By publisher

2. By title

3. By issue number

Most collectors and dealers will often first categorize a comic by its publisher. The two major publishers of comics that are most often collected are Marvel Comics and DC Comics. Comic books are often arranged in retail stores and advertised by publisher. This makes it easier to locate a comic book if you know that it was published by Marvel Comics, for example, or by DC Comics, or by one of the many other comic book publishers.

After the publisher, the next important category is the comic's title. All the Marvel titles, for instance, will be kept with all the other books published by Marvel. Usually these titles are organized in alphabetical order according to publisher.

Every comic book also has a unique number or issue. The first issue is usually marked *#1* on the cover or inside the comic, the second issue is #2, and so on. Within each comic title, the issues are arranged in numerical order, usually from #1 to the latest issue number.

Of course, there are many other ways to organize and identify a comic book, but the majority of collectors, dealers, and advertisers use this three-fold system of *publisher, title,* and *number.*

Okay, now how do you determine the publisher, title, and number of a comic? Fortunately, you can usually do this just by looking at the cover.

Sometimes, however, the cover of a comic may not have this information. Particularly some of the older comics and those from certain publishers will not have the number on the cover. And in some cases, the title on the cover of the comic is not the official title recognized by collectors.

In these cases, you'll have to identify a comic book by reading its *indicia.* The indicia of a comic book are usually printed at the bottom of the comic's first page, or they may be on the inside front cover of older comics. The title given in the comic's indicia may not be the same as the title on the cover. In this case, the official title is always the one listed in the indicia and not the one on the cover. The indicia also give such information as the comic's publisher, the number and date, and sometimes the editor and other publishing information. If you're ever in doubt, the indicia almost always have the correct information about the comic. The cover sometimes is misnumbered or mistitled.

You'll also notice that the date of the comic appears on the cover and in the indicia. This date rarely makes any difference in identifying a comic. Collectors generally ignore the month and year that a comic was published; instead, they use the title and issue number alone to identify a comic.

Collecting by Numbers

Many collectors like to collect by numbers. That is, they start off trying to get every issue of a comic, from #1 until the last or current issue.

If the collector can get every issue of a comic that has been published, then he has a *set* of that title. A set is just a complete collection of a particular title, with no missing numbers.

Sometimes a collector may not have a complete set of a title but may have most of the numbers, such as #1 through #10, or #3 to #26, or whatever. A collection of consecutively numbered issues of a comic title is called a *run*. For example, if you own issues #4, #5, and #6 of a particular comic, then you have a small run of that title. Collectors usually start out with a run of a title and then try to build it into a set by buying issues that are missing from their collection.

Collectors try to complete sets or a run of comics because either they want to read all the issues of a particular title or they just want to say that they have a "complete" collection. Collectors, no matter what they collect, often want to have a complete set, and it's no different with comic books.

Condition of a Comic Book and Its Value

Collectors also pay a lot of attention to the condition of their comics. They want them in as nice a shape as possible, and they want to preserve them in the state that they are in. A good-looking comic will always be worth more than the same issue in poor condition. Collectors, like most other people, want their possessions to look nice and to be complete.

It's important to take care of the comics you collect so that you will be able to sell them easily and for more money when it comes time for you to get rid of them. There is a whole chapter in this book on taking care of your collection, but for right now we'll tell you how to handle a comic book properly so that it won't become damaged.

When you read a comic book, be careful that you do not pull the cover or fold it around the book. Hold the comic flat and supported in one hand and turn the pages with the other hand. Don't fold or crease the cover or any of the pages. Store the book carefully when you're through reading it and away from any possible damage. A good collector not only organizes his collection but protects and preserves it for the enjoyment of future collectors who may someday buy his comic books.

The beginning collector is often confused about comic book condition grades, such as *Good, Fine,* or *Mint.* Since being able to determine the condition of a comic is so important to the collector, there is a chapter on how to grade your comics. In addition, you'll discover how the condition of a comic affects its value. For right now, just realize the importance of taking care of your comics so that they will stay in good condition and be worth more should you ever decide to sell them.

How to Become an Expert

The more you know about comics, the more fun you'll have and the better collection you'll be able to put together. Collectors and investors do more than just buy and save comic books. They spend a lot of time studying them, finding out about the people who create the comics, and learning about the comic marketplace.

How do you become an expert on comics? The first step in comic book education may be as close as your neighborhood comic shop, so let's go!

The Comic Book Store

In almost every major city there is now at least one comic book store. These retail bookstores specialize in new and old comic books for the collector, and they can often be located in the Yellow Pages. If there is not a comic shop in your hometown, there is probably one in a large city near you.

The beginning collector can get a good education in collecting comics just by visiting one of these stores on a typical Saturday. There you'll be able to meet other comic collectors and get to see all the new comics that have just come out. You'll also be able to look at back issues of comics and discover titles that you never knew existed.

In addition, you'll be able to buy books, magazines, and newspapers devoted to comic collecting. Some stores also carry supplies that a beginning collector needs for his hobby, such as comic book price guides, indexes, comic book storage boxes and bags, and so forth. You'll also get to

12

talk with the comic store's employees, who are probably collectors themselves. In this way, you can start your informal education and pick up a
lot of tips.

Comic book stores are excellent places to buy new comics for your
collection, since they often stock every title that is published. By giving
your business to your favorite comic book store, you can develop a good
relationship with the owners and employees, who will be able to help you
build your own collection.

Learning from Other Collectors

The quickest way to find out more about comic collecting is to spend
time around other collectors and fans. Besides meeting and talking to
collectors in comic book specialty shops, you can also join (or start!) a
comic book club in your hometown. Quite often, you can get a school,
library, or community organization to donate a meeting place for your
club. Get the word out to other local collectors that a monthly club is
forming, and hold meetings where you can trade, buy and sell, and talk
about comic books. The quickest way to get an in-depth education on
comic books is to talk with experienced collectors.

Perhaps it may be difficult for you to start a local comic club if there is
not already one. If so, you'll want to make plans to attend one of the
biggest meetings of all—the comic book convention.

The Comic Convention

For a comic collector, there is a heaven on earth, and it's called a comic
convention.

At a comic convention, you will see hundreds of thousands of old and
rare comics for sale. You'll meet other fans and collectors who share your
interests. You'll get to talk to the artists and writers who create your
favorite comics, and you'll be able to buy, sell, and trade comic books 24
hours a day.

Comic conventions are now held in almost every major city at least
once or twice a year. Typically there may be more than 1,000 conventions
a year, including the small local gatherings as well as the regional and
nationwide conventions. You can find these gatherings of comic book
fans, collectors, dealers, and professionals in almost every state.

The major national conventions are usually held in New York, Chicago, Atlanta, and San Diego. At these conventions, past and present
comic book professionals meet with fans and participate in panel discussions, autograph sessions, and convention parties.

Going to a convention is easy. Just find out when one near you is
scheduled by checking with local comic book stores or national collector

publications. Most of the conventions are held during the summer, but on any given weekend there are more than a dozen such gatherings somewhere in the country.

There are three main reasons for going to a convention: (1) to buy, sell, and trade comics, (2) to meet fans, collectors, and comic book professionals, and (3) to gain more knowledge about the comic-collecting hobby.

One of the biggest thrills of attending your first comic book convention is seeing thousands of old comics for the first time. You'll see rarities, first issues, and back issues of your favorite titles. You'll discover new comics that you may want to collect. You may find that one special issue you've been wanting for years.

A comic convention usually lasts for two or three days, although one-day comic shows are also becoming popular. There are activities around the clock at a good convention. You can attend panel discussions and listen to the professionals in the comic field, go to costume parties and banquets, watch old movies, talk and visit with other fans and collectors.

Three days at a large comic convention are equal to three years of collecting comics by yourself. If you've never been to one, promise yourself that this year you'll attend your first convention.

Collector Publications

Talking with other collectors and going to conventions are a lot of fun, but you probably won't have the chance all that often. Most of the time, your contact with collectors will be through the pages of magazines and newspapers published for comic fans. These fan-oriented publications are called *fanzines*—short for fan magazines. Fanzines are usually written and published just for fun by comic collectors and fans.

Comic fanzines often have interviews with comic artists and writers, reviews of current comics, news about upcoming comics and new issues, in-depth studies of older comics, and ads for older comic books and other fan publications. There are also letter columns in the fanzines, news about past and future comic conventions, and reports on comic sales and circulation figures.

If you want to become an expert, fanzines are absolutely, positively required reading. There are at least four or five major fanzines published each month. Some of the collector newspapers come out every week, and there are hundreds of collector publications that appear infrequently and irregularly throughout the year.

It is impossible to buy comics intelligently for investment or resale unless you study the fanzines. The fanzines reflect collector interest. They indicate which books collectors are buying and which artists can make a book a bestseller. Simply by reading the ads in a fanzine, you can develop a real feel for the current comic marketplace. You can tell which comics are selling well and which comics people are eager to buy.

There are a few fanzines that have been published regularly for five or ten years. Most, however, have a short lifespan. Often, a fanzine appears for only one issue, or only two issues per year may come out. A few of the longer-publishing fanzines are listed in the Appendix. You can also get the current addresses for many fanzines from some of the major collector publications, which are also listed in the appendix. And don't forget that your local comic book specialty store will also have a good stack of new fanzines, comic indexes, and other collector publications that are required reading for the beginning collector.

The Price Guide

And that brings us to perhaps the most valuable source for the collector's education—*The Comic Book Price Guide,* edited by Robert M. Overstreet. This book is published every year and is available in most bookstores around the country. Almost every comic book that has been published in the last 50 years is listed in this book, along with its current value.

In addition to price information, other important collecting data are given, such as the major artists who drew the comics, notes on special collector's issues, introduction and origins of popular characters, and so forth.

The guide also gives the market trends for the previous year, as well as investor's data for the comic marketplace.

There are other price guides for comic books, but Overstreet's *The Comic Book Price Guide* is the one most commonly used by collectors and dealers. The book is often called "the Overstreet price guide," and it is the most complete single reference book on the entire comic field. If you purchase no other book on comic collecting, this guide is the one to get.

Using a Comic Book Price Guide. When you first start collecting, it's sometimes hard to see where your collecting will take you or even to know what to collect. You may not know which issues of a comic you need, or you may not be aware of certain titles or special editions. You may not know who published a specific comic or when it was issued or how much it is worth. This is why the beginning collector should buy the latest issue of *The Comic Book Price Guide.* In the guide, you can find virtually every comic published, in alphabetical order. Each entry in the guide also has such information as the comic's publisher, date of first and last issues, any special collector information (such as the artist who drew the comic), and a list of prices for each book.

Here's a sample listing from such a price guide:

Green Hornet Comics
Feb. 1967–No. 3, Aug. 1967
Gold Key

	Good	Fine	Mint
1	2.00	6.00	12.00
2,3	1.50	4.50	9.00

Notice that the title of the comic is listed first. Under the title is the date that the comic was first published (February 1967) and the number and date of the last issue (#3, August 1967). Beneath the publication dates is the name of the publisher (Gold Key). Finally, each issue of the comic is listed, along with its value in a specific condition. In this example, issue #1 is estimated to be worth $2 in Good condition, $6 in Fine condition, and $12 in Mint, or brand-new, condition.

Issues #2 and #3 are listed on the same line because they have the same value (that is, both #2 and #3 are worth $1.50 each in Good condition, $4.50 in Fine, and $9 in Mint).

By reading a price guide, you can quickly find out which comics are the most valuable and which ones you may want to collect.

Other Books on Comics and Collecting

Until the late 1960s, there were very few books written about comics. Much of the published work on comic art before that time concentrated on the newspaper comic strips. Comic books just weren't taken very seriously until Jules Feiffer's book *The Great Comic Book Heroes* was published in 1965. The book was excerpted in *Playboy* magazine, and suddenly comic books became "in." Comic book heroes began appearing in the new Pop Art posters and paintings of the mid-1960s. Articles about comic books appeared in scholarly journals and popular periodicals. And then the nation went comic book crazy.

Batman and Robin roared across our television screens in an immediately popular TV series that not only became a top-rated show but was soon shown twice a week. In the next ten years, books on comics appeared every few months. There were collections of old comic strips, histories of comic books, encyclopedias on comic books, and more reference material on comics and their creators than had been published in the entire preceding 30 years of comic book history.

In the past several years, most of the important books on comics, especially collections of comic book reprints, have been published by independent fans and collectors for the specialized comic book marketplace. This means you'll usually have to obtain these books either directly from the publisher or through comic book specialty shops.

However, there have also been a significant number of books on comics and collecting comics from some of the major publishers, and these books can be found in libraries and regular bookstores. A listing of the general-interest books on comics and comic collecting can be found in the Appendix.

Talking Like a Collector

"Did you see that direct-sale book from Marvel with the X-Men reprints on Baxter paper? It's got the debut of Marvel Girl, with a cameo of the Hulk and a crossover appearance of the Avengers. The pencils really aren't that great, but the book has a knockout splash page, with some pretty decent inks and layouts. And even though it's a one-shot, I think it's going to be a hot book."

Huh?

You can hear such dialogue at a comic convention, comic book store, or wherever comic collectors and fans gather. Like other hobbies and specialized interests, comic collecting has its own vocabulary that sets it off from all other worlds.

I remember asking one woman at a convention if she had any "precode Atlas horror comics with Everett artwork." She looked at me as if I'd just asked for a moon fossil with ketchup on it. She shook her head and told me, "You'll have to wait until my husband comes back. He sells these things. I don't understand comic book talk."

It does sometimes seem that comic collectors need an interpreter when they talk to people in the "ordinary world." Comic book collectors, like people in any other specialized field or hobby, have a vocabulary of their own to help them discuss their interests in great detail. For instance, do you know what the title on a comic cover is called? It's a *logo*. Collectors can talk about a particular comic's logo without having to say, "You know—that thingamajig on the cover."

While this specialized language can be helpful when you're discussing comic books, it can be awfully confusing to someone who doesn't know the lingo. To round off your quick introduction to comic collecting, here's a vocabulary list of some of the terms used most often by comic collectors and fans. Some of these words may still not make much sense to you until you get involved in a conversation with another collector. For right now, just scan this glossary and get a feel for "collector talk."

A Glossary of Collector Terms

back issue   A previous issue of a current comic book, or any issue of an older comic that is no longer being published.

back-up story   The first story in a comic is called the *lead* story and usually features the main character or is the longest story in the book. If there are any other stories in the comic, they are called back-up stories or back-up strips. Sometimes back-up stories feature characters other than the main character; they may also be shorter than the lead story.

B&W   Black and white. Usually refers to magazine-size comic books printed without color.

Baxter paper   Very-high-quality paper that does not deteriorate as quickly as the regular paper used in printing comics. Baxter paper is thicker and slicker and allows higher color contrast than normal comic paper. Introduced in the early 1980s, Baxter paper is usually reserved for high-quality, collector-oriented publications.

BLB   Big Little Book. In the 1930s, before comic books achieved wide popularity, comic strips from the newspapers were published in a small book format. Some comic collectors also collect Big Little Books as part of their hobby interests.

cameo   A limited appearance by another character, usually only for a few panels or one or two pages. Different from *crossover* (*see below*).

cel   An original painting on celluloid that makes up one frame of an animated cartoon.

code   *See* Comics Code and precode.

colorist   A person that specifies which colors are to be used when a comic book is printed.

Comics Code   The set of regulations that a comic book must conform to in order to be approved by the Comics Magazine Association of America. This voluntary organization is supported and funded by the comic industry and serves as a self-censorship board. Comics that pass the standards are allowed to display the CMAA seal of approval on their covers.

con   *See* convention; *comicon* is sometimes used to distinguish a comic book convention from a science-fiction gathering.

convention   A gathering of fans, professionals, dealers, and collectors to buy, sell, trade, discuss, and appreciate all aspects of the comic book field.

crossover   A major appearance by a character from a different comic book, usually for several pages or the entire issue.

dailies   Daily newspaper comic strips.

dealer   A person who sells comic books, comic strips, original art, and related comic items.

debut   The first appearance of a comic character; not necessarily the same as *origin*.

direct sales   Comic books that are sold directly from the publisher to the retailer, bypassing the traditional magazine distributor. Direct-sale books are sold on a nonreturnable basis. Since most stores that buy on a direct-sale basis are comic book specialty shops, *direct books* is often another name for comics aimed specifically at the comic collector and serious fan as opposed to the general comic reader.

fandom   A general term that applies to the network of all comic fans, collectors, dealers, fanzines, and all people interested in comic books for enjoyment.

fanzine   A specialized magazine for collectors and comic fans.

first appearance   The first time a comic character appears in any story or book; not necessarily the same as *origin*.

flashback   A retelling of a story or character's origin within a comic book story.

four-color   Refers to the four-color process used in printing comic books, in which four basic colors are used to produce all the shades used in a comic book. May also refer to a series of comic books published by Dell Comics from 1939 to 1962.

funny animals   A term that refers to humor and "funny" comic titles, such as Mickey Mouse, Donald Duck, *et al.*

giveaway   A comic book or pamphlet that was given away free as advertising or promotion.

GOH   Guest of honor; the featured speaker or guest at a comic convention.

Golden Age   A period of comic books, roughly from 1938 to 1947, that saw the birth of the major comic book publishers, titles, and characters.

Good Girl Art (GGA)   Pin-up-type art usually found in comic books from the late 1940s through the early 1950s that was designed to appeal to young men of that time.

grading   Determining the condition of a comic book.

hot   A term used to describe a comic title that is selling very well or whose back issues are in demand by collectors.

illo   Short for *illustration*. May be used as a noun, such as *spot illo* for a small illustration, or as a verb, as in "illoed by Jack Kirby."

independent comics   Comics that are published by one of the smaller publishing houses instead of the traditional, major comic publishers.

inker   An artist who goes over the penciled drawings for a comic book in ink; the inker may often also draw the backgrounds and other fine details of a story.

intro   Introduction; such as "intro Superboy" to mark the introduction of that character into a story or title.

key issue or number   A comic that is especially valuable or essential for a collection. For example, any comic that introduces a major character or is a #1 issue or features an appearance by a major artist could be called a key issue.

layouts   The preliminary sketches for a comic book strip or page that serve as a guideline to the penciler, who refines these rough drawings.

lettercol   The letter column in a comic or magazine.

letterer   The individual who letters the word balloons in a comic and the sound effects of a comic panel ("POW! KA-WHACK! ZINNNNG!").

limited series   A comic book title that has a predetermined number of issues. For instance, a limited series may have only three, four, or twelve issues. A limited series is usually devoted to one popular character or concept. Such series are popular with collectors because they are easy to collect as a complete set.

logo   The title design on the cover of a comic book or story.

Mando paper   High-grade paper that is of a better quality than the traditional paper used to print comic books. Not quite as thick or glossy as Baxter paper, Mando paper is nevertheless less acidic and less prone to deterioration than the traditional newsprint that most comics are printed on.

one-shot   A special one-issue-only title, such as a collection of comic stories or a major feature.

origin   The beginning or creation of a comic character. Usually a story that details the past history of a character in the comic and how he came to be. Not necessarily the same as the character's first appearance, and not necessarily in the first issue.

original art   The actual artwork drawn and inked by one or more artists for a comic book page or comic strip. Original artwork is usually done in black and white (no coloring) and in a larger size than it is eventually printed.

Overstreet Refers to Overstreet's *Comic Book Price Guide* prices or condition-grading system. Examples: "Priced below Overstreet" indicates that the comic is selling for less than its value in the Overstreet price guide. "Graded by Overstreet" indicates that the grading standards outlined in the Overstreet price guide were used to determine the book's condition.

panel A single drawing enclosed within a border or frame that is used in sequence to make up a comic strip or comic book page.

penciler The artist who pencils the characters and some of the background of a comic book or strip.

precode Refers to comics issued before 1955, the year that the Comic Book Code took effect. Precode comics were generally more violent and more "adult" and were censored only by the publisher itself. Although technically any comic book published before 1955 is precode, the term is usually applied to comics from 1949 to 1954, particularly those dealing with crime, horror, and mystery.

pulp A magazine from the 1920s through the 1940s, generally printed on cheap paper and devoted to science-fiction, mystery, horror, western, romance, and adventure genres. Many comic writers originally wrote for the pulp magazines, and several comic companies also published pulp magazines during the 1940s.

reprint A reissue of an original comic book or the reprinting of a story from a comic book.

revival The bringing back of an old comic character.

run Two or more consecutively numbered issues of one comic book title. Collectors often try to complete runs of comics, such as the first 20 issues or the last 50 issues.

SASE Self-addressed, stamped envelope. Usually requested by comic book dealers when you write to them for information.

scripter The writer of the comic book story.

SF Science fiction.

set A complete collection of a particular comic book title, from its first issue to its last or current issue.

Silver Age A period of comic books beginning roughly in 1959 and lasting until the late 1960s. So called because many of the characters from Golden Age comics were revived for new comics during this period. Most comic book historians date the beginning of the Silver Age from the publication of *Showcase #4,* which contained the first costumed hero revival (the Flash) from the 1940s.

SOTI *Seduction of the Innocent;* the title of a book published in the early 1950s that detailed various violent and sexual excesses in comic books of that time. Comic books that were singled out for criticism in the book are often referred to as "Seduction books," or "SOTI issues."

splash panel A large panel, usually one-half to a full page, that is often used to mark the beginning of a comic book story.

strip A sequence of two or more panels; usually refers to a comic strip in a newspaper or magazine.

sub Subscription. Sometimes used to describe the condition of a comic, as in "sub issue," which means that the comic has been mailed folded to the subscriber.

Sunday page The colored comic strips from a Sunday newspaper; usually refers to an entire page, which may or may not contain more than one comic strip. Early Sunday pages often had only one strip per page.

swipe An imitation or even a tracing of a piece of comic artwork by another artist.

underground Comic books published by alternative publishers that usually explore controversial topics such as drugs, sex, politics, religion, and cultural values. Underground comics are free of censorship and were originally part of the counterculture youth movement of the late 1960s and early 1970s.

THE MANY WAYS OF COMIC COLLECTING

You can't get them all. There, I said it, so you can just relax now.

Every comic collector's dream is to someday own a copy of every comic book published. Dreams die hard, but put this one to rest. Nobody will ever be able to assemble the ultimate, complete comic collection. There are far too many comics for any one person to track down, buy, and catalog.

But that should be welcome news, because now you can collect comics all your life and still not reach the end. But it also means that at some-time or other, you will have to decide which comics you do want to read and collect. Defining your collection, picking your interests, then me-thodically assembling the kind of collection you want is one of the great-est joys of comic collecting.

Every collection is different. Some people collect only one company's comics, such as all the Marvels, or all the DC comics. Others specialize in comics drawn by a certain artist, while some collectors are content to get every issue of only one particular comic title.

To the beginning (and advanced) collector, the choices are overwhelm-ing. Within a single month, you can buy over a hundred different new comic book titles. Simply keeping up with every comic published in one year can reach up into the four-figure price range.

And if you look past the new comics and start to think about all the back issues and hundreds of thousands of older comics that are waiting to be read, stored, and treasured . . . well, as I said, just relax. You can't have them all, but you can build your own individual collection of comics that will give you years of pleasure.

This chapter tells you about the many different ways you can collect comics, how to specialize, how to define your own interests, and how to add comic-related collectibles to your collection as well.

The Beginning Collector

The beginning or young comic collector should start out by collecting as many *new* comics as he can afford. New comics are readily available and inexpensive and can be collected on a month-by-month basis as they appear on the newsstands. Equally important, new comics are always sold in mint condition at a standard retail price. This means that the inexperienced collector will not have to worry about comic book condition grades or variable prices for older and rarer issues.

After you have read a wide variety of new comics for three to six months, pick out a few titles that you especially like. At this point, start to search for recent back issues of these titles. You can often find issues of your favorite comic that are six-months to one-year old for a low price, especially if you go to used bookstores, flea markets, or garage sales. Quite often a comic book store or comic book dealer will have recent back issues for sale for about the same price as a new comic.

After a few months of reading and saving the new comics and recent back issues, you'll start to have definite favorites. Maybe you'll like a particular character or a special artist or even all the comics by one publisher or another. At this point, it's time to start specializing.

Specializing means that you decide to collect one type of comic in preference to other comics. By specializing, you can have more money to spend on your favorite new comic titles as well as older issues of those titles. This doesn't mean you can't buy other comics that are not part of your special interests, but it does allow you to concentrate on the comics that you are most interested in.

As you specialize and build your collection of a few selected titles, keep reading as many other new comics as you can. You may discover other books that you'll want to add to your collection, and you may decide to stop collecting certain titles as the months go by.

Whatever you do, keep this one rule in mind: Collect only what you yourself enjoy.

After you've been reading and collecting the new comics for a year or so, you'll probably start to wonder about all the other comics that have been published in the last 50 years. Now you can slowly start to add the older and more expensive comics to your growing collection. You may discover that you like the older comics better than the new books that appear each month. If so, just collect the older comics and read the new comics that you still like.

A beginning collector, however, should first collect the comics that are being published *now*. Collecting current comics is an inexpensive way to start your collection, and it can help give you an appreciation for the entire field and history of comics.

Don't be in too great a hurry to specialize and narrow your collecting interests. At the beginning, it's a good idea to read as many different types of comics as you can so you'll have a general appreciation of the comic book art form.

The Older Collector

The older collector who is starting out may not be at all interested in the new comic releases. Very often the older comic collector starts collecting because he remembers the comics that he read when he was young, and he wants to get those same issues again.

In this case, you may start collecting by first buying inexpensive issues of comics that you read several years ago. Don't be in a hurry to buy the real rarities or the #1 issues of comics from your childhood. First buy some copies of comics that you remember enjoying most as a child. No matter what your age, you can always find relatively cheap comics from the period when you were growing up.

After you've gotten a year or so of collecting experience under your belt, you're ready to start buying more expensive issues that you want. Collecting back issues of older comics is a lot different from starting off by collecting new comics. Older comics are more difficult to locate and more expensive, and they also require that you know about comic conditions, price guides, grading standards, and so forth in order to make an intelligent purchase.

Nothing is more satisfying, however, than finally locating that old comic book you remember fondly from 10, 20, or 30 years ago. Building a collection of only back-issue comics requires a little more care and effort than starting off with the new issues, but you have one distinct advantage over most beginning collectors: You already know which comics you want to collect.

The Different Methods of Collecting

Okay, you've made a good start. You've been collecting new or older comics for several months, and now you feel it's time to specialize. There are many ways to collect comics that will give your collection order and meaning. Let's look at the more popular methods that other collectors use to define their comic collections.

Collecting by Title

Most people start collecting comics by trying to get all the issues of their favorite comic title. It's an easy way to collect; you just try to get one copy of every issue of a certain comic. This way of collecting is called *set collecting*. A set is simply all the issues of a specific title.

Set collecting can be easy or difficult, depending on how many issues of a comic were published. For example, a long-running title such as *Superman* or *The Fantastic Four* has several hundred different issues, some of them very expensive. On the other hand, there are other comics with only five or six issues published, and such a set might be easy to complete. In the early 1980s, comic publishers realized that collectors often like to collect by sets, so they started issuing limited comic book series that usually have only four, six or twelve issues in the set. These limited series are easy to complete, since the collector can buy each new issue as it appears on the newsstand.

Of course, you don't have to collect *every* issue of a certain comic if you collect by title. Many collectors that concentrate on a long-published title may collect only specific issues or avoid the high-priced issues in a set, or they may start their collection not with the first issue of the title, but with the 50th issue or the 100th issue. This way they don't have to spend a lot of money for the earlier and usually more expensive books.

Such collectors are said to be collecting a *run* of a comic title. A run is several consecutive issues of the same comic, such as #5 through #12 or #125 to #200.

Collecting by titles, sets, or runs is an easy and satisfying way to start collecting. For one thing, you always know which numbers you need to have a complete collection. By concentrating on a run or set of a comic title, you can also follow one character or story line for a number of issues.

From collecting by title, it's a short step to collecting by character. For example, suppose you collect the comic *The Amazing Spider-Man* because you like to read about the Spider-Man character. In this case, you'll probably also want to collect the other comics that feature Spider-Man. Here's how one collector described her experience when she started collecting by a specific comic title or character:

> *Like most, my collection has gone through a lot of changes. My original collection was just a big box of all the Marvel comics that I had read for five years. I sold it when I moved. After a few years of life without comics, I picked up an old copy of* Strange Tales *with Steve Ditko's Dr. Strange.*
>
> *I was hooked again, but this time I collected only comics with the character Dr. Strange. After I completed the* Strange Tales *run that featured Dr. Strange, I branched out to collecting* all *the comics with Dr. Strange appearances—even one-panel cameos and all the crossovers. This meant that I bought back issues of such comics as* The Defenders *and any other Marvel comics that had Dr. Strange stories.*
>
> *This passion for having a complete Dr. Strange collection lasted for three years. By the end of that time, I had every comic published from 1963 to 1980 that had Dr. Strange stories, appearances, or strips. My*

collection was finally complete—and then I started on Spider-Man. Do you have any idea how many comics he has appeared in? Ask me again in ten years. Maybe I'll have them all by then.

This fan's collecting experiences are the same as many other beginning collectors'. Quite often, a comic reader becomes totally fascinated by one character. This fascination sparks an interest in collecting *every* comic that character appeared in. And so, quite innocently, a mildly interested comic reader is transformed into a fanatical comic collector.

From collecting a single character or title, it's an easy step to expand your interests to *all* the titles published by that particular company. At this point, the collector is no longer a Spider-Man or Superman fan, but a Marvel or DC collector. And that brings us to the next way that collectors organize their collections and collecting interests—by publisher.

Collecting by Publisher or Comic Company

The great comic collectors' debate is always over which publisher produces the best comics. If you want to start a fight, walk into a crowded comic store on a busy Saturday and yell, "Marvel [or DC] comics stink!" Soon you'll be busy defending yourself from enraged supporters of one or the other comic company.

Collectors often describe themselves as Marvel collectors or DC collectors or EC collectors or of whatever comic company or publisher they admire most. It is fun and challenging to collect comics by publisher. You can concentrate on getting most or all of the new issues released by that publisher, and you can seek out the many older titles published by the company.

Collecting according to publisher allows you to become familiar with a group of artists who work for the same company. You also get to know the many different characters that are owned by a specific publisher, and you can collect all the comics that your favorite characters appear in. Collecting by comic company also gives your collection a uniform appearance and a sense of order and purpose.

Some people who collect comics according to publisher may become *completists*. A completist is a collector who wants a copy of *every* comic issued by a company. Some completists are satisfied with simply buying every new issue that a company publishes, while others also want every back issue as well. Needless to say, being any type of comic book completist takes a lot of time, effort, and money. But if you've got the collecting fever, sometimes nothing less will do.

Collecting by Artist

Many comic readers have a favorite artist or artists. Quite often, they want to collect as many comics as possible drawn by that artist.

Collecting by artist is a popular and satisfying way to learn about comics and their creators. Since a popular artist's work is rarely limited to one title or even one comic company, you'll probably have to collect a wide range of comics if you specialize by artist. This can turn into a real treasure hunt as you seek out the more obscure material by such prolific artists as Steve Ditko, Jack Kirby, and Bob Powell. Even the newer comic artists, such as John Byrne or Frank Miller, have stories and strips published in enough different comic titles to give the dedicated collector plenty to collect.

When you collect comics by artist, you develop a deep knowledge of and appreciation for the people who created the comics. You can become an expert on an artist and follow his career over the years in several titles and different publishers. Eventually you may learn enough about the artist so that you can share your knowledge with other collectors.

For example, one fan in California is collecting all the comics that have artwork by Gene Colan, an artist that has worked for both DC and Marvel comics. "I consider myself the world's foremost expert on Gene Colan," the collector said.

> *I specialize in finding unknown works by Gene Colan and am on my way to completing an index to all the man's work. The fun thing about collecting this way is that I'll discover some comic or the other that contains art by Colan that no one else is aware of.*
>
> *For example, when I was digging through a box of comics at a convention recently, I ran across a copy of* Two-Gun Kid #7. *Not your usual hot item, right? But inside was a story that sure looked like early Gene Colan work to me. So I bought the comic and mailed it to Colan himself to help me positively identify it for my index. That's the fun in collecting —unearthing and making known the works of the various artists.*

Collecting by Comic Type

Besides collecting comics by title, character, publisher, or artist, some collectors specialize in certain types of comics, such as costumed hero comics, western comics, romance comics, science-fiction comics, or whatever. This is called collecting by type or category.

A type collector will buy and collect any comic that fits into the general category he is interested in. Although most comics today are the costumed hero type, comics published during the first 25 years of comics were also likely to be western comics, crime comics, horror comics, "funny-animal" comics, humor comics, and so on.

Collectors that collect by category pick out a general kind of comic that they like to read—such as war comics or romance comics. They then buy as many comics of that type as possible, regardless of age, publisher, or artist. Collecting by type can allow you to specialize yet still assemble a wide-ranging and representative comic collection that covers many years and companies.

Collecting by Time Period

Most collectors have heard of the Golden Age of comics (those comics published in the 1940s) and the Silver Age of comics (those from the early 1960s). There are definite eras in the history of comics, and each period has its own type of comics. Since the history of comics spans over 50 years, most collectors select a specific period that they collect comics from.

For example, one collector may collect only comics published from 1961 to 1967, while another may want comics issued only *after* 1980. Collecting by time period is an interesting way to organize your collection because you have definite starting and stopping points. You don't have to worry about getting comics that fall outside the specific period you are concentrating on.

You can set any limits you want on the period you decide to collect. One collector I know collects only comics that were published when he was a kid, from six to twelve years old, or in his case, the period from 1964 to 1970.

Other collectors may specialize in comics issued during World War II (1941–1945), or the Golden Age (1939–1949), or the Silver Age (1959–1967), or just any arbitrary time range. One person I know is collecting only comics that were issued during his year of birth, 1949. He estimates that after five years of collecting 1949 comics only, he still needs 2,000 more, so it can be a real challenge to collect a specific time period.

Collecting by Cover

Comics have colorful covers, and some collectors specialize in comics according to the cover content alone. For example, one collector is collecting comics that have patriotic cover themes, which were very popular during World War II. Another collector is assembling a collection of comics that feature trains on the cover.

One popular way of collecting by cover is to specialize in "infinity" comic covers. An infinity cover shows a comic character holding an issue of a comic, and on that cover of the comic is the same character holding an issue of the same comic, and so on.

Cover collecting allows you to express whatever particular interest you might have, and it can give your collection a distinctive personal touch. For example, a dentist friend of mine has put together a comic collection with covers that feature dentist chairs, dentists, or prominently displayed teeth!

Collecting by Numbers

Of course, one of the most popular methods of collecting is to collect as many #1 issues of different comics as possible. Since #1 issues often increase in value more quickly than other issues, this is a popular approach for investors to take. Of course, not all #1 issues are valuable, and since there are about 17,000 different comic titles, there are plenty of #1 issues for you to collect.

Another popular variation on collecting first issues is to collect the #100 issue of comic titles. And some collectors specialize in collecting the *last* issue of a discontinued title.

Collecting by Content

Another way of organizing your collection is to collect comics that have a certain theme. For example, some collectors specialize in comics from the early 1950s that feature excessive violence, sexual innuendo, bondage, or fetish themes (and you thought comics were just for kids!).

Other collectors may seek out comics that have religious themes or overtones, such as the Catholic giveaway comics of the 1950s or the Treasure Chest comics. Still other collectors want comics that feature political propaganda or famous personalities. For example, several comics in the early 1960s had appearances by the Beatles in their pages, and these are collected by both comic collectors and Beatles fans.

Collecting comics by their content alone is enormously challenging, because you don't know if a comic will fit into your specialized collection until you actually read it.

It may sound like collectors are very organized and methodical people that sit down and decide what they want to collect. In reality, most comic collectors stumble into their collecting method, and very often they use a combination of two or more of the approaches discussed here. For example, you could collect comics from a certain time period that were published by a specific company and that featured art by one particular artist. A collector in Kentucky, for instance, collects only books published by Charlton Comics from 1956 to 1959 that have stories by the artist Steve Ditko.

Perhaps you'll never define your collecting interests so specifically, and that's good. Part of the fun of collecting is that you can collect whatever you want, and you should never pass up a book just because it doesn't "fit" into your present collection. Who knows? It may be the start of a new collection!

Actually, most advanced collectors do have several different collections going at once. For instance, they may have a small collection of comics from the 1940s, a set of Marvel comics from the 1960s to the 1980s, and a representative collection of horror comics from the 1950s as well.

There are many, many ways to organize your collection, besides the major methods outlined here. You're only limited by your imagination and particular interests. So go ahead—collect what you like. It'll probably fit in somewhere, somehow.

Is There Life Beyond Comics?

Comic collecting is not just comic books. There are hundreds of related items, books, artwork, and comic strips that collectors include in their collections. If you collect comic books, someday you'll find yourself adding other comic-related collectibles to your accumulation. Let's take a look at other items that collectors are interested in besides the regular comic book.

Original Art

Comic books and comic strips are printed from the original art done by the artist. This original artwork is usually done in pen and ink on bristol board and is one and a half to two times the size of the printed page. For each page in a comic book, there is a page of original black-and-white artwork.

Collectors collect original art because it is a one-of-a-kind item. There may be hundreds of thousands of an issue of any particular comic book, but only one copy of the artist's original artwork was used to produce the comic.

Owning a piece of original comic art is exciting because it is a piece of comic history that was drawn by the artist's own hand. There are comic book dealers who specialize in selling original comic art. They get the original artwork either directly from the artist or from other collectors or from the publisher. Some of the artists who work for the comics also sell their artwork directly to individuals after it has been used for printing the books.

Although several thousand pages of original art are produced each month for new comics, the prices for artwork by the more popular artists can still be relatively high. Some artists are reluctant to sell their original work, and the competition is fierce for the truly outstanding pieces of original comic book artwork.

Still, even the beginning collector on a budget can afford the more modestly priced pages of comic art, and inexpensive sketches can often be purchased directly from an artist at a comic convention.

31

Hanging a piece of original comic book art on your wall can really showcase your collection and provide an interesting conversation piece for collectors and noncollectors alike.

Foreign Comics

Comic collectors often forget that comic books are not published in their country alone. Almost every country in the world produces some type of comic strips or comic books. These foreign comics add a distinctive flair to your collection, and they can even be a good source of reprinted American comics.

Comics published in Great Britain, Italy, and the Netherlands are particularly good sources for American reprinted comics. Often you can find current foreign comics that reprint American comic strips and stories from 20 to 30 years ago. These other countries also produce their own unique and beautiful comic books.

Quite often, these foreign comics may be better produced, drawn, and colored than their American counterparts. Japanese comics, for example, are sometimes hundreds of pages long and treat adult themes not seen in American books. Spanish comics use the romance-horror genre extensively, while Australian comics have heroes that could give Batman or the Fantastic Four a good fight.

Having a few foreign comics can give your collection an international flair and give you an insight into other people's customs, languages, and values.

Newspaper Strips

A very close relative to the comic book is the daily newspaper comic strip. In fact, newspaper comic strips are the grandparents of today's comic books. Some comic book collectors like to clip and save daily and Sunday newspaper comic strips, or they may collect books that reprint these strips.

Collecting comic strips can be very inexpensive, yet a real challenge. Some collectors subscribe to several newspapers from around the country just so they can get their favorite comic strips. Other collectors search through antique stores and bookstores for newspapers 30 or 40 years old that have strips they are interested in.

Collectors and dealers sometimes advertise daily and Sunday newspaper comic strips for sale by monthly or yearly lots. For instance, you could buy one or two months' worth of daily Dick Tracy strips from the 1940s, or a full year's worth of Sunday comic pages with Prince Valiant from the 1930s.

Besides the original newspaper comic strips, collectors look for books that reprint such strips. Fortunately, in the last several years there has been a trend to collect and issue more and more collections of the classic newspaper comic strips in inexpensive collector's editions.

The newspaper comic strips of the past often featured art and story lines that were superior to many comic books, and they deserve a serious look by the comic collector.

Big Little Books

A cross between a comic book and newspaper strips, Big Little Books appeared in the 1930s and featured a comic strip panel on one page and text on the opposite page. BLBs, as they are often referred to by collectors, usually featured well-known comic-strip characters such as Buck Rogers, Popeye, Mickey Mouse, Dick Tracy, and Little Orphan Annie. The Big Little Books are relatively inexpensive, compared to the old comic books, and they may sometimes be found in antique shops and used bookstores, as well as from some comic book dealers.

Gum Cards

You may be familiar with bubble-gum baseball cards, but did you know that there were many other gum cards that featured comic book characters? Some comic book collectors also collect gum cards from the 1940s through the 1980s that have comic strip characters, TV personalities, and other nonsports characters. Some of these gum cards were even drawn by comic book artists, which makes them a definite comic collectible.

There are hundreds of other comic-related collectibles, such as toys, games, portfolios, movie posters, and even video tapes, all of which collectors include in their general collections. Having these items can accentuate your comic collection and provide you with hours of pleasure as you explore life beyond comic books.

But for some collectors, comic books are enough. In fact, they can't seem to get enough. And that's what the next chapter is about: how to get the comic books you want.

HOW TO FIND AND BUY COMIC BOOKS

The hunt was on. My two comic-collecting friends and I were driving down a back country road, looking for—what else?—comic books.

"There's the auction sign at that farmhouse up ahead. Pull over, pull over," one of my friends said.

We got out and wandered among the old farm equipment, quilts, antique furniture, and boxes of junk that were being auctioned off that day.

"All right!" one of my companions yelled. We ran over to an old trunk. There they were. Almost a hundred old and brightly colored comics from World War II—The Human Torch, Captain America, Batman, Wonder Woman.

We pooled our money and waited for the trunk to come up for bidding. Two hours later, we were splitting up a $5,000 comic collection that we'd bought for $45. It was a good day.

One of the biggest thrills of comic collecting is making the "big find." Even if you don't run across old and valuable comics, it's almost just as much fun to find that new comic you've waiting to read or buying that one issue you need to complete your collection.

No doubt about it. Finding and buying comics is a collector's favorite pastime—second only to reading the books.

And there are many ways to build your collection, to get your favorite new books, and to find old and rare comics. That's what this chapter is all about: how to get comic books!

Getting New Comic Books

The easiest way to build a collection is to buy new comic books as they appear on the newsstands. Until a few years ago, most comic collectors got their new books from a local store or magazine rack.

Today, there are other, better ways to collect new comic books. There are three major sources for new comics:

1. The local newsstand,

2. Mail-order firms and new-issue services, and

3. Specialty bookstores that sell primarily comic books and science fiction.

Comics from the Newsstand

Some years ago, a comic book reader could walk into any drugstore, grocery store, or newspaper stand and find every issue of every new comic book published. Today, that's not true.

In the last ten years, comic book distribution through normal outlets has greatly decreased. Many stores are phasing out the low-priced comic book. Stores that still carry comics rarely have a complete line. Some titles are never received. Issues may be skipped from one month to the next. You might find issues four months out of date, and you may never see a special comic that you have been waiting for.

When the comics do arrive at the local store, they may be put in racks and quickly become bent or damaged. Finding comics in like-new condition is hard at most retail stores.

Not only that, but comic publishers are now selling some of their titles only by direct mail or to specialty stores. These comics are often called *direct-only* titles and are sold mostly to the collector's market and not to the casual comic reader. Many new and independent comic companies sell their comics only to collector's markets and specialty stores. You'll never see these direct-only and independently produced comics at a newsstand, and it's often these books that have the most interest for the collector.

So there are a lot of disadvantages to getting new comics from a newsstand or store. If you live in a small town, however, this may be the only way you can get in person the comics you need. If that's the case, then you should find out from the store manager when the comic books are delivered. They usually arrive once or twice a week, with the other magazines.

When you find out which day the comics arrive, show up as early as you can and buy the books you need before they become damaged or are sold to other readers. If you make friends with the store manager, you can request that he get certain comic titles for you. You may have to shop all over town to get all the new titles you need. But there's a better way.

New Comics by Mail

You can always subscribe to a comic book directly from the publisher. But you probably shouldn't. Subscription comics from the publisher are often bent, folded, or damaged in the mail. In the old days, comic publishers folded the books firmly in half before they mailed them to subscribers. Folded and damaged comics are almost worthless to a collector, so you do not want to subscribe directly from the publisher (unless you just want to read and not save the comic; in this case, a subscription is fine).

There is, however, another and better way to get new comics by mail. You can join a new-issue subscription service that is offered by several mail-order businesses. A new-issue subscription service works like this. A store or a comic distributor buys hundreds or thousands of every new issue that comes out. Each month or every two weeks, these subscription services send out a list of the new comics that will be available that month. When you get the list, you check the books you want and how many issues of each. When the comics arrive from the publisher, the service sends you a box of all the new comics by mail.

You can also tell the subscription service you want to receive every new issue that comes out for a particular title or that features a certain character. Then you'll get the books automatically as they are issued. Some collectors place a standing order for all #1 issues, for example, and that way they are assured of getting the valuable first issue of a title.

Usually these independent subscription services charge a modest fee for postage and handling if your monthly order is small. In return, you'll get new comics that are shipped in a strong box for protection.

Most of the time, these subscription services will pay postage and packaging costs on moderate-size orders, and for most orders you can even get discounts on these new books. With these discounts, you'll end up paying less for the comics than if you'd bought them directly off the newsstand. For example, almost all subscription services offer new comics to collectors at a 20–25-percent discount no matter how many comics you order. And if you're purchasing a lot of new comics each month, you may be able to get them by mail at a savings of 50 percent or more! Not only do you save money, but you may even get the new comics by mail a week or two before they hit the local stores.

So there are many advantages to using a new-issue subscription service for comics. The only disadvantage is that you do not get to see the comic before you buy it. As a result, you may buy a comic that you would not want if you had seen it first. Still, a comic subscription service may be just for you.

Now, how do you find a good subscription service? It's useless for me to give names and addresses of the independent businesses that offer this kind of service, because new ones are always appearing and old ones may be gone by the time you read this. Several of these subscription services, however, regularly advertise in the comic book price guides and in other magazines devoted to the comic-collecting hobby, including comic books themselves.

A good subscription service is invaluable to the collector who lives away from a large city. For those collectors who live near a large business and retail center, there may be an even better way to get the new comics.

New Comics from Comic Book Store

Imagine walking into a store that has nothing but thousands and thousands of comic books lining the walls, covering the floor, and spilling out of dozens of boxes. This would have been impossible a few years ago, but today hundreds of comic book specialty stores have appeared all over the country. If you live in or near a major city, you probably have a local comic book store near you.

These comic shops, often called "specialty bookstores," are the best place to get your new comics. Why? Because comic book stores usually carry a complete line of all comics published. They make sure that the new comics stay in "new" condition. They get the new titles and #1 issues in large quantities. They will often save for you the comics you need. And they can often point out new books and titles that you may want to read.

Besides all that, these stores carry other materials for comic collectors, such as storage boxes, protective bags, price guides, books about comics, and other related goodies. The stores and their owners are fantastic sources of information for the new collector. You will also meet other collectors buying their comic books there, and some of these stores have a friendly "clubhouse" atmosphere that welcomes comic fans.

Possibly there may be no such store near you. If not, then make a real effort to visit one when you travel to other cities. These stores are usually listed in the Yellow Pages under "Bookstores," and they also often advertise in the comic collector's magazines and price guides.

The only disadvantage to buying new comics from specialty stores is that very popular titles often sell out quickly. If collectors feel that a certain new comic will become very valuable in a few months or a few years, then they may descend on the store and buy up all the issues for investment. Store owners, too, may suddenly pull a rapidly selling title for their own backstock so that they will have back issues to sell later. The only solution is to have a standing order with the store so that they will reserve specific issues for you.

Finding Old Comics

Buying the latest issue of your favorite title is always fun, but the real thrill of collecting comes when you find that old and rare, never-before-seen comic book. Turning up old comics can be easy or a real challenge, depending on how much money you want to spend. You can get the rarest comic in the world tomorrow—if you have a few thousand dollars. You can also build a large collection of back-issue comic books for less than the cost of new comic books—if you work hard and don't mind waiting for bargains.

Let's look at the different ways you can find old comic books. We'll start with the cheapest way and work on up to the most expensive (and easiest) method of building your collection.

Friends and Relatives

When you first start collecting comics, tell as many of your friends and relatives as you can. Many times they will have old comics from their childhood or from their children, or they may often run across these books and save them for you.

Many of your friends may read or have read comic books but may not collect them. Often they will give you their old comics for less than they paid for them.

The trick is this: Make sure that *all* your family and friends know you want old comic books. Many collectors have built large, valuable collections just from the old books given to them by their friends and family.

Your Local Community

In almost any town there are used bookstores, thrift shops, garage and rummage sales, flea markets, antique shops, and so on. Visit all the stores that may have old comic books. Many times these local stores will sell their recent back comics at about half the cover price. These are excellent places to find the valuable issues published in the last two or three years.

You can find really old comics in such places as well. Last year, for example, I found 500 old comics from 1942 to 1948 in an antique store. They wanted about a dollar each for old comics that were worth $5–$25 apiece. (And yes, I bought them all.)

Not only should you visit every such store in your town or nearby, but you should also read the classified section of your local paper. Look for auctions and estate sales where old comics may turn up. You can also run a small ad in your local paper, advertising that you buy old comic books.

Many times there are people in your hometown that have old comic books but don't know where to sell them. If you run an ad in the paper (WANTED: Old comic books. Quick cash.) you can be sure that you'll get at least a few inquiries.

Some enterprising collectors print up circulars or business cards to advertise that they are in the market for old comic books. They leave these cards or circulars at flea markets, antique shops, laundromats, or wherever people gather. You can sometimes buy comics that you find this way for a fraction of their true value since these people are interested in disposing of their old comics for any reasonable price.

With a little work, you can still find in your own town hundreds of back-issue comics at prices cheaper than the new issues. So get going, and good luck!

Other Local Collectors

No matter where you live, you'll find other people interested in reading and collecting comic books. You should make friends with these fellow collectors and help each other with your collecting. You can trade back issues with these people, exchange information, and add greatly to your fun. Talking about old comic books with other collectors is probably the most enjoyable aspect of the hobby. Not only that, you'll discover that you can get many books you need from other fans, as well as getting rid of extra comics from your own collection.

Often local collectors will form comic clubs. These clubs can be sponsored by a school or other community center so you can have a free place to meet and conduct your trading sessions. Local collectors are one of the most enjoyable ways to find old comic books, and it's also quite inexpensive.

Comic Book Conventions

A comic book convention is a local, state, or national gathering of hundreds or thousands of comic book collectors, fans, and dealers. Almost every major city in the country now has at least one such convention a year. These get-togethers are an excellent place to find back issues of comics.

One of the biggest thrills of attending your first comic book convention is seeing thousands of comics that you never knew existed. You'll see rarities, first issues, and back issues of your favorite titles. You'll discover new comics that you may want to collect. You may find that one special issue that you have been wanting for years.

- Before you spend any money at all, try to see what is generally available. Make a quick tour of the "dealer's room" (the usual name for the large area where people are selling and buying comics at a convention) and decide who has the best books for the best prices.

• After you've found a dealer with some of the books you want, compare his prices and grading with a current price guide. Make sure he isn't charging too much for his books.

• After you've found a few comics at prices you like, ask the dealer if you may examine them more closely. This means taking the book from its protective bag and looking at the inside pages for signs of age, wear, or damage. Be especially careful and check the book for missing pages, coupons, and panels. If you discover several days later that you bought a damaged comic at a convention, it may be impossible to locate the dealer to return the book.

• When looking at comics you wish to buy, always treat the books very carefully. Don't bend the books or put them back in the wrong place. Dealers don't mind your browsing through their stock, but do so with consideration.

• After you have selected several comics to buy, total up their prices. You may be able to get a 10–20-percent discount if you're buying a lot of books. You can always ask for a discount or make an offer that is somethat less than what the dealer is asking. Some dealers are very willing to bargain, and you may end up saving a substantial sum by just asking. Don't expect discounts on small purchases of one or two books, however.

• After you buy the comics, place them carefully in a protective envelope, bag, or box or a briefcase. Have your name and address written somewhere on this package. It's very easy to set a bag of recently purchased comics down at a convention and lose it. If the book is very valuable, you may also wish to get a receipt or some other proof of purchase.

One word of warning: Decide before you go to a convention how much money you can afford to spend. In the excitement of the moment, it's very, very easy to spend your entire yearly budget for comics in about two hours. Also, try to hold back a few dollars until the very end of the convention. This is the time when dealers are willing to bargain, since they would rather sell a comic than pack it up to take it back home.

Mail-Order Dealers

Depending on where you live, you may have to purchase all your old comic books by mail. This is also an excellent way to get needed books. Remember, however, that you sometimes pay a little extra for mail-order books because of postage and handling costs.

There is an advantage, though: You can find almost any book you would ever want if you buy by mail. A majority of the back-issue comic business is still done by mail. Even dealers who have retail comic book stores still do a respectable amount of buying and selling through the mail. In the early days of comic collecting, almost all collections were built by placing mail orders.

So, where can you find these mail-order dealers? Some of them advertise in the comic books themselves. You can also find hundreds of them advertising in such books as *The Comic Book Price Guide* and in the pages of collector publications such as *The Comics Buyer's Guide*.

Once you have found a mail-order dealer, there are several things you should know before you place the first order. Here are the basics for ordering comic books by mail:

- Before you buy, compare prices. You can end up paying five times as much for a comic book from one dealer as you would from another dealer. Mail-order dealers will charge whatever they think they can get for a comic book. There can be a major difference in prices, and you're foolish if you send your money to the first dealer you find. Try to get several lists at one time. Pick out two or three books you're interested in, then compare prices for these books in all the lists. You'll notice that the books, besides being priced, have their general condition indicated. The condition, or grade, of the comic determines how much it is worth.

- The next step is to place a sample order with a dealer. This means that you send him a small order for some of the books you want—not for all that you need. You should place a sample order for three reasons: first, to make sure that the dealer is honest and still in business (the vast majority of comic book dealers are very honest and friendly people); second, to see how accurately he grades his books (after all, if the comic books are overgraded, they're not worth the price being asked); and third, to judge his service (how fast he ships your comics, how well they are packaged, and so on).

You should place sample orders with at least three different dealers to find the best. At this point, you can reorder from your favorite dealer, but you should also send off for lists from still other people selling comics by mail. Once you have found a dealer you like and trust, you can give him more and more of your repeat business. You can tell him what books you're looking for, and he may be able to help you. When you want to sell your comics, your regular mail-order dealer may buy them from you.

A friendly, reliable comic dealer can help you build your collection, and it's worth the time and trouble to find a good one.

When you order books by mail; do the following:

• Pay by money order (obtainable from a post office or store) or by check. This way you have a record of the money you sent. Do not send cash. If you pay by personal check, your order may be delayed for two to three weeks while the dealer waits for the check to clear your bank.

• Next, print your name and address on your order form, on your letter to the dealer, and on the envelope. You want him to know where to send your books, so make sure your address appears at least twice, in case any one piece of correspondence is lost.

• The dealer may be sold out of the books you want, so you may want to list alternate choices he can send you. If you do not want any alternate choices or a credit, ask for a refund for any comics that may already have been sold.

• Allow at least two to three weeks for you to receive your order. Sometimes it may take up to six weeks to get your comics if the mails are slow. If you haven't received your books after five weeks, write a polite note to the dealer and ask him where your comics are. Repeat the order information you sent, if possible. If you receive no response after another two weeks, then you should send one more letter to the dealer and another letter to the magazine or book that he advertised in. After a two-month delay and no response, you should contact the post office to file a complaint. Most dealers, however, are eager to please you and will try to get your comics to you as soon as possible (usually within three weeks if you pay by money order).

• It's a good idea to have your order sent to you insured in case it gets lost in the mail. During the 15 years I've sold comics by mail, three packages have been lost (and that's out of over a thousand packages sent). Still, when you order by mail, save a copy of your order and request insurance (it may cost an extra dollar). This way you should have few problems in ordering comics by mail.

• Most reputable mail-order dealers have a liberal returns policy. This means that if you are not satisfied with the comic in any way, you can return it for a full refund. The only good reason for returning a comic, however, is that it was not in the condition advertised or that there were defects in the comic not noted in the ad. If you're going to return a misgraded comic, send it back within three to five days after you get it. Insure the package for the full value of the comic and send a letter to the dealer ahead of the package, telling him that you are returning the comic.

Buying and selling comics by mail is still the backbone of the collecting industry. And besides, nothing can match the excitement of opening a large package of comics that was just delivered to your front door.

Buying Old Comics from Retail Stores

Although comic book stores and specialty shops are the best place to buy your new comics, they are not necessarily the perfect place to purchase old and rare comics.

Comic book stores have an overhead. There are rent and salaries to be paid. Only a standard profit can be made from selling new comics; therefore, many specialty comic book stores often must charge full collector value for their old comic books.

Usually a comic book store also enjoys a type of monopoly since there may be only one or two such places in town. As a result, the prices on old comics do not have to be as competitive as those at some mail-order dealers.

There is, however, a big advantage to buying old and rare comics from an established store. You get to see the book before you buy it (not usually possible with mail order), and you can be assured of satisfaction.

Then, too, a comic book store can help you find certain books you may need. They'll also stand behind the authenticity of the book that they sell. So there are very good reasons to buy back issues from a regular comic book specialty store. Just remember, however, that you will probably pay a moderate premium for this convenience, which is only fair.

The Art of Buying Comics

There really are an art and a science in buying old comic books. Sure, you can just plunk down your money and take your chances, but with a little thought you can save some money, have some fun, and build your collection up very quickly. Let's look at some of the mechanics of purchasing comics.

Ready for Inspection

"Check this comic out," a manager of a local comic store told me as he laid a beautiful, mint comic on the counter. The comic was 40 years old, but it looked as though it had been printed yesterday.

"Nice," I said, "but how much?"

He quoted me a price that was about one-tenth its market value. "What's the catch?" I asked.

"Look inside," he replied.

I flipped through the old comic until I came to the next-to-last page. There it was. A coupon had been cut out, ruining the last story of the comic.

"A beautiful book with an ugly mistake. I'll have a hard time selling it," he said as he put the comic back under the counter.

When you buy a comic, never judge a book by its cover. You have to inspect older comics carefully before purchasing them. A missing centerfold, a scribbled-on page, or a torn-out coupon can mean real disappointment when you get the book home to read it.

Few dealers have the time to inspect every comic that comes through their hands, unless it is an expensive issue. It's up to the buyer to inspect the comic first to make sure that it is complete and undamaged.

Actually, after several years of collecting, you will be able to tell if a comic has a missing page or centerfold just by picking it up. Comics with one or two missing pages feel lighter to the experienced collector. To make sure, however, always at least check to see if the centerfold is still in the comic before buying it.

Newer comics too must be carefully inspected before purchase. A bumped corner, bent spine, or creased page turns a new Mint comic into a new Near-Mint comic, which is worth less. Some collectors go to extremes, however; I've seen some comic readers examine over 30 copies of a new issue, carefully comparing each one to the next for such mundane details as exact centering of staples and tight color registration.

If the comic represents a substantial investment, however, you had better give it a close inspection before handing over your money.

Handling a Comic

When you inspect a comic for purchase, you'd better know how to handle it properly, or the book (and yourself!) may become damaged.

First, if the comic book is inside a plastic bag that is taped closed, remove the tape completely from the bag. Don't leave the tape edges sticking up on the comic bag, or the book may get caught on the exposed sticky tape.

Now slide out the book gently into one hand, and immediately position one hand under the book so that you are fully supporting the comic's back cover and spine. Take care that you do not bend or crease the comic in any way as you remove it.

Now, holding the comic's spine in one hand, turn the pages of the comic with the other hand. At all times, keep the comic from being pulled back, and avoid placing any stress on the comic's staples.

After you've examined the comic, you may put it in back in the bag, or very often the dealer will want to place it back inside to make sure that it is not damaged. If you put the comic back into its protective bag, make sure that no corners become turned up or bent as the book is slid back in. Once the book is inside its bag, check that the spine is not rolled and that no corners or covers are curled inside the bag. Replace the removed tape, and put the comic book back in exactly the same location where you found it.

Do not assume that you can take any comic you're interested in from its protective bag. Always ask the dealer first if he minds you removing the comic for inspection or whether he would like to do the honors himself.

Be courteous and considerate when examining a comic book. After all, if you don't buy it, it must stay in good shape for the next collector.

Discounts and Bargaining

Most retail-store dealers won't be able to give you much of a discount on new comics. The price is already fixed by the publisher and distributor. It's like asking for a discount on new clothes or weekly groceries. It's just not done too often with new comics, unless you're buying in bulk from a subscription service.

Bargains and discounts, however, are very common for back-issue comics. Comic dealers have more of a margin to work with when they buy and sell back issues. For example, a dealer may be asking $5 for an old comic, but in reality, he may have bought it for 50 cents. In this case, he can afford to bargain on the book's price and still make a good profit.

If you're buying any significant number of back-issue and older comics, you have a perfect right to expect some sort of price break. Usually the dealer won't offer you a discount, but if you ask for one, you may get the books for less than the asking price.

How much of a discount should you expect? It depends on how hungry the dealer is, which comics you're buying, and how many you're purchasing. Generally, you should be able to get 10–20 percent off your total purchase. If you're buying really slow-moving titles in large quantities, a dealer may be happy to let you have them at half price, just to make room and get some quick cash.

It's generally easier to bargain face to face than through the mails. Cash on hand is a powerful argument, although you may be able to get books cheaper through mail-order dealers by making a counteroffer.

The important point to remember is this: There is no such thing as a firmly fixed price on a back-issue comic. Prices fluctuate, interests change, and the comic market moves on. It is not an insult to the dealer if you offer a price lower than what he is asking—provided that the price is not ridiculously lower. Most comic dealers would rather sell a book for slightly less than they are asking for it than to have it sit on their shelves for another month or year.

Don't be shy. Bargain. Ask for discounts. After all, you are the one with the money to spend, and believe it or not, even comic book dealers like money more than they do comics.

Overpriced Comics

A danger for the beginning collector is buying comic books that are priced above their true market value. The most common reason for this is that the comic books have been overgraded by the dealer. This kind of mistake can be easily avoided by learning how to grade a comic correctly and by looking up the current value of the comic in the price guide.

However, both beginning and experienced collectors may still pay too much for a comic simply because it is overvalued in a price guide. In other words, the estimated price for a comic in a price guide may be far above the actual market value of the book.

For example, in 1971 DC Comics published the first issue of *Mister Miracle* comics which was drawn by Jack Kirby, who had been the major artist at Marvel Comics for the previous ten years. Kirby had developed and drawn such popular comics as the Fantastic Four, the Avengers, and Thor for Marvel, and it was assumed that his new work at DC would be equally popular with fans and collectors.

The first issue of *Mister Miracle* by Kirby did indeed capture the imagination of collectors in early 1971. During the same period, Kirby also started several other new titles and characters for DC Comics, and interest boomed in these new comics. *Mister Miracle #1* was soon selling for $3 per copy, and Kirby collectors, as well as both Marvel and DC fans, wanted the first issue of the book, especially after the series had been going for eight or ten months.

The price for the first issue went to $4 by early 1976, then to $4.50 the next year, and finally up to $6 by 1979. By 1980, however, collectors were no longer interested in the Kirby DC comics from seven or eight years before. Those collectors that remembered and still wanted the first issue of *Mister Miracle* already had their copies. There was not enough new interest in the book among younger collectors.

The result? Copies of *Mister Miracle #1* became difficult to sell, and there were far more copies than there was current demand. By 1980, the price for the book had dropped from $6 to $4.50. Even at the reduced price, the book still never sold as well as it did during its first two years.

A comic can become overpriced in a price guide simply because it reflects a *past* demand for the book that has not been adjusted to the true market value. Once a comic has reached a certain price level, it is difficult to lower it in the marketplace. Nobody wants to sell a book for less than he paid for it. Consequently, if the book's value does decrease, there is a built-in resistance to selling it for a lower price.

The book's price is kept artificially high by both dealers and collectors. Most people would rather keep a comic than take a loss on it. As a result, you'll always be able to find plenty of copies of an overpriced comic for sale, but when it comes time for you to sell the book—well, good luck.

How can you tell if a book is overpriced for the marketplace? First, if the comic is offered for sale on many different price lists and by many different dealers, then you can assume that there is a plentiful supply. If you see a wide range in the prices being asked for the book, then you know that there is no firm market price for the comic, and you may be able to bargain or get it for less.

Finally, you can talk to other collectors. If very few fans are interested in collecting back issues of a comic or if the particular character or artist in the comic is no longer popular, then the book may be overpriced.

Don't always assume that simply because a certain price is given for a comic in a price guide or dealer list or ad that the book is automatically worth that much. Comics do get "stuck" at an inflated price, and it may take several years for the price to readjust itself to the true, lower market value.

Also, yesterday's bestsellers have a way of becoming tomorrow's turkeys. Collectors are fickle, interests change, and titles wax and wane in popularity. If a book's price gets fixed too high, don't be afraid to make a reasonable counteroffer. If the dealer is knowledgeable, he'll probably accept it and get rid of a slow-moving, overpriced, and difficult-to-sell comic.

Underpriced Comics

Collectors hate overpriced comics, but not as much as they love finding a book that is priced below its true market value. One of the biggest thrills of comic collecting is to discover the hidden bargains that still exist in undiscovered and underpriced books.

A comic may be underpriced in a guide, list, or advertisement for two reasons:

1. The price guides and lists have not had a chance to catch up with the rapidly increasing collector interest in a particular title or book. (This is usually true for recently published comics, new titles, or new artists.)

2. Collectors have not yet discovered the true worth of the comic. (This usually applies to older, unusual, or minor comic titles that have not attracted a lot of previous collector interest.)

The official comic book price guides are issued only on a yearly or semi-yearly basis. For the few extremely popular comics, this is not often enough to reflect the true market value. A comic may double or even triple in price in one or two months, especially when it first "takes off."

For example, let's look at the price increases for a mint copy of *X-Men #94* from 1977 through 1981:

X-Men #94 (First Issue with the New X-Men; Marvel Comics)

Year	Mint Value
1977	$0.30
1978	$0.60
1979	$3.75
1980	$5.25
1981	$60.00

In late 1978, I sold a copy of *X-Men #94* to a dealer for $1. I thought I was getting a good deal; after all, the price for it in the current guide was only 60 cents. The dealer knew, however, that a lot of collectors were looking for the book. He was able to sell it for $2.50 with no trouble. The book was "hot," and its price was jumping faster than price guides and price lists could keep up.

I learned my lesson. During 1980, I bought as many copies of *X-Men #94* as I could find, and I gladly paid the full guide price, which was $5.25 at the time. Suddenly I discovered that there were no more copies to be had at that price. Even though the price guide said they were worth $5.25, the books started selling for $10, then $20, and finally $40–45. By the next year, the book was worth $60—almost 12 times its previous value.

With that type of book, you could have paid five times the comic's guide price and still made a respectable profit. The book was a classic example of the underpriced, recently issued comic.

How can you spot such underpriced comics? The easiest way is to get a feel for what is currently selling on a month-to-month basis by going to comic book shops and regional conventions. Talk to the dealers and other collectors. Find out what people are buying and talking about. Study dealers' lists and ads from month to month. See whether certain comics are difficult to find and whether their prices slowly edge up every month or two. Picking out the new comics that are currently underpriced takes a lot of skill, a thorough knowledge of the current comic market, and a reasonable helping of dumb luck.

A second type of underpriced comic, besides the hot new issues, is the older, yet-to-be-discovered collector's item. For example, in 1979 you could buy a mint copy of *Action #267* from 1960 for $4.50. It was priced the same as *Action #266* or *#268*.

Now let's go to 1984, five years later. *Action #266* and *#268* have increased a moderate amount to $12 each. But now the price for a mint copy of *Action #267* is a whopping $100! What happened in four years that made this one comic eight times as valuable as similar issues?

Quite simply, collectors discovered that *Action #267* contained the third appearance of the Legion of Superheroes, a popular and widely collected team of comic characters. That particular issue then became much more sought after, since there was an enthusiastic group of collectors who wanted comics with the Legion of Superheroes.

If you had known that the Legion appeared in *Action Comics #267* back in 1979, then you probably would have realized that the comic was underpriced. Had you bought 50 issues of the book at that time, even at full guide price from dealers, then you would have made almost $5,000 profit five years later on a $250 investment!

An older comic may be underpriced in a guide or dealer's list simply because collectors are not yet aware of the contents of the book or which artist appeared in the comic. There are still many comics with artwork by popular and widely collected artists that are undiscovered and thus underpriced.

The best way to find the older, underpriced comics is to seek out back issues of miscellaneous and rarely collected comics and look for artwork by artists in demand. Once you learn to recognize an artist's work, you may be able to discover other underpriced comics. Also, keep your eyes open for special issues that feature a character's origin or a change in story line. As these special issues are discovered by other collectors, their prices will also increase dramatically.

Finding and buying comics is a major part of collecting. There's more to it than giving your money to the first person who has a few extra comic books. Since you have only a limited amount of money to spend on your interests, it's important that you learn to comparison shop, bargain, and hunt for comics in out-of-the-way spots. A true collector is not content simply to buy and trade comics that are already in the collector's marketplace. He goes out and discovers new collections and new sources for old comic books.

So go forth. Explore and seek after the elusive comic. May you be lucky enough to make the "big find" and humble enough not to brag—too loudly.

CONDITION, SCARCITY, AND VALUES OF COMIC BOOKS

Have you ever wondered why old comic books are hard to find? The truth is that many comics are damaged, destroyed, or discarded within a few years of being bought.

Comic books are printed on inexpensive paper and held together by two staples. The covers of a comic don't really protect the book, and the comic is usually read so that the cover and interior pages become torn, creased, and chipped. The paper the comic is printed on is not meant to last more than 30 or 40 years, even under ideal conditions.

And old comics are rarely stored under ideal conditions. Most were tossed into garages or attics or boxes in closets. There they decayed from heat, humidity, and insect attacks.

Comics that survived in good condition became rarities, and those in better shape brought higher prices.

Comic collectors are no different from any other type of collector. They want their collectible comics to be in the best possible shape, to look "nice." A comic in good condition will also last longer than a book that has been mistreated.

Some collectors are not so concerned about the condition of their books. They're more interested in reading and enjoying the comic instead of trying to find one that is in perfect shape. All collectors, however, prefer a comic that is in better condition to one that is in poor shape.

It's important that you know how to determine the condition of a particular comic book that you want to buy or sell. For one thing, a collector or dealer uses the condition of a comic to identify and describe the book. If you want to buy and sell intelligently, you need to understand what other collectors are talking about when they describe a comic's condition. And besides that, the condition of a comic book can affect its value so much that you could very easily lose or spend too much money on improperly graded comics.

This chapter tells you how to determine the condition of a comic and how condition affects the price of a book.

The Different Conditions of a Comic Book

Every comic book can be described as being in one of the following conditions: Mint, Fine, Good, Fair, or Poor.

A *Mint* comic book is "brand new." It looks as though it's just been printed and fresh off the newsstand.

A *Fine* comic book has been carefully read, stored, and protected. It has some signs of wear and reading, but it looks sharp, or "fine."

A *Good* comic book may have some creases, folds, or minor tears. Yet it is completely intact with no major defects or damage.

A *Fair* comic book is the typically used and well-read comic.

A *Poor* comic book has suffered major damage, such as badly torn pages, chunks missing from the cover, and covers torn loose, and shows heavy signs of aging.

Most collectors will not buy a comic in Fair or Poor condition. The price guides for comic books usually list prices for only three major categories: Good, Fine, and Mint.

Collectors also split these three grades into other condition categories, such as *Very Good, Very Fine,* and *Near Mint.* For example, a comic book that is better than Good but less than Fine is labeled Very Good. Similarly, a comic better than Fine but less than Mint may be called Very Fine or Near Mint. In addition, books that are perfect in every way are labeled *Pristine Mint.*

Learning How to Grade a Comic

How can you tell if a comic book is in Fine or Mint condition? What's the difference between a Very Good comic and one that is only Good? The most difficult part of collecting comics is learning how to grade a comic correctly.

A good portion of grading properly is knowing how to recognize the various defects and damages a comic book may suffer and how these defects affect its condition rating.

For example, a Mint comic should have no defects, no signs of wear or tear, and no signs of damage through reading or handling, regardless of its age. A Fine comic may have a few minor defects and signs of wear, while a Good comic, although well-read and worn, is still a complete and solid copy.

The first step in determining a comic book's condition is to examine it closely for any signs of wear, damage, or other defects.

To help you determine the condition of a comic, all the possible defects that a book may have are listed below in three categories:

1. Printing defects

2. Age defects

3. Wear defects

After some of these defects are listed and discussed, we'll see how to determine the condition of a comic based on these defects.

Printing Defects

Printing defects are something the comic is born with. A comic when published may have its cover stapled off-center, or it may be missing a staple, or the staples may not be in line with each other.

The cover may be printed so that a white edge shows on one side while the other edge is wrapped around the spine. The cover and the interior pages may be printed off-register, so that lines are superimposed over the coloring. Some color plates may have been inadvertently missed in the printing, making the book appear strangely or unevenly colored. The pages may be printed out of order or uncut so that they must be torn to be read. Occasionally, the interior pages of a book may not match the cover.

Printing defects are rarely so serious that they affect the grading of a comic by more than a half grade; in fact, printing defects are usually only considered when grading Mint or Pristine Mint books, which demand total perfection in all respects. (Remember that a comic graded as Pristine Mint is totally perfect with absolutely no defects or signs of wear or aging.)

Although not strictly printing defects, two other injuries a comic may suffer before it even reaches the reader are arrival dates stamped or penciled on the cover and color coding on the top edge of the book. These are actually distribution defects since they are caused by the distributor of the comic book. Distribution defects, like printing defects, usually affect only the Mint or Pristine Mint grades. Here's what these distribution defects consist of:

- **Arrival Dates.** Although it's no longer common practice, newsstand dealers and distributors used to stamp on a book the date the comic was placed on the stands. This way they knew when to remove it, after a month or so. Sometimes the date was penciled on the cover. Most collectors don't consider these to be serious defects, unless the comic is being graded as Near Mint or better. Arrival dates are facts of life for some of the older books, and they are accepted as normal in the lower grades.

- **Color Coding.** Another practice used by distributors to date the arrival of the books is to spray the top edge of the comic pages with a colored ink. Comics received one week may have a red edge, while the next week's batch may get a green inking. Inked comic edges always downgrade a book to at least Near Mint, since they are considered a slightly worse defect than a stamped arrival date.

Again, you don't have to be too concerned with printing defects unless you are grading a book better than Near Mint.

Aging Defects

Comic books do not age gracefully. And while it is not quite correct to call damages incurred by natural aging "defects," collectors must take into account the ravages of time, temperature, humidity, and storage when grading a comic.

Comic books pass through seven stages of aging, as determined by the *color* of the interior pages. Each stage is worse than the previous state of aging and affects the overall condition of the book as described below:

1. White pages. When comics are brand new, they have white interior pages. White pages indicate that the acids in the paper have not yet started to cause the book to deteriorate. Mint and Near-Mint–to–Mint books must have white pages.

2. Off-white pages. As comics age, the pages begin to turn from white to yellow. Books in Very Fine and Very Fine–to–Near-Mint condition must have pages off-white or better.

3. Light yellow. Gradually the off-white pages of a comic turn light yellow, especially along the margins of the book. As the pages first begin to yellow in the margins, the book is only in Fine condition.

4. Dark yellow. Eventually, the yellowed margins of a comic spread until the entire page is completely yellowed and the margins themselves have become a dark yellow. By this time the book is only in Very Good condition.

5. Light brown. After a book is yellow, it starts to turn brown in the margins. Lightly browned margins and interior pages place a book only in the Good category. Once a book starts to brown, its aging process accelerates, and steps must be taken to preserve it from rapid decay.

6. Dark brown. If a browning comic is not deacidified (see chapter 6, "Taking Care of Your Collection") or stored under the best possible conditions, it will gradually turn a darker and darker brown. Once

the pages have turned dark brown, the comic can only be considered to be in Fair condition, regardless of how nice the rest of the comic may appear.

7. Brittle. The final stage of an aging comic book. The pages are now starting to chip and crumble when turned. The pages are very dark brown in the margins, especially along the edges and near the spine. Once a book is brittle, it is in Poor condition and should never be stored with comic books in better condition. Brittle books are highly acidic and will hasten the decay of any nearby comics. Keep brittle books by themselves in a plastic bag and use them only as reading copies.

All too often, dealers and collectors will ignore the aging defects of a book. Simply because a book has no obvious tears, creases, or handling defects does not mean that the comic is in nice shape unless the interior pages are also free from yellowing, browning, brittleness, or other age defects.

On the other hand, a book can still have perfectly white pages and be free from aging defects, yet may be in only Fair condition if it has major tears or heavy spine wear, or what are commonly called *wear defects*.

Wear Defects

These are the most common type of condition defects suffered by a comic and what most collectors look at when they determine a comic's grade. Wear defects occur when a comic is read, handled (or mishandled), and stored.

Remember that until only within the last 20 years, comics were treated very casually by readers. They were likely to roll a comic up and stick it in their back pocket, turn the cover back around the spine when reading it, or toss it into the bottom of a cluttered closet. The books were also often traded, sold, resold, and passed around until they finally fell apart from continual rereading. Such is the fate of well-loved and well-read comics.

Let's look at the injuries a comic can incur when in circulation, in order from minor to major defects.

Minor Wear Defects. Minor wear defects are usually light creases along the corners of a comic or wear along the book's spine. Some small wrinkles, scuffing, and minor spotting are also allowable minor defects.

- **Spine wear.** Just reading a comic will begin to wear the spine. The repeated opening and closing of a comic book places a strain on

The inside of a well-stocked comic book store. These specialty bookstores are a rich source of materials for both the new and experienced collector.

Comic book stores and dealers at conventions often display their more valuable comics under glass.

Comic fanzines are published by collectors and are an important source for information about old and new comics, and the people who create them.

Foreign comics are an unexplored and rewarding field for most collectors. Besides the original strips done in other countries, American comics such as this first issue of Spiderman comics are often reprinted.

Most comic book stores and dealers arrange their old comic books according to publisher and title in a series of storage boxes.

Arrival dates were often stamped, penciled, or inked on comic covers by the distributors so that the books would be pulled after a certain date if they had not been sold. Not a serious defect, but it should be noted on comics graded in Near Mint to Mint condition.

Although not a serious defect, an off-centered staple is a printing defect that can prevent a comic from being in perfect condition.

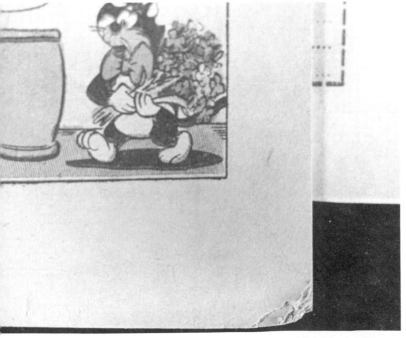

The comic on the top shows dark brown aging and developing brittleness on the corner of the book. The second comic behind, while not as severely aged, shows the beginnings of yellowing.

This comic shows signs of minor spine and cover wear where the comic was rolled around while being read. Such minor wear is acceptable on a book in Very Good to Fine condition. Note also the off-centered staple, about ⅛ inch from the spine.

Spine wear, as pictured here, is a common wear defect. In this example, the wear is heavy enough so that the comic could only be considered to be in Very Good condition at best.

An extreme case of "spine split" or spine damage on an older comic.

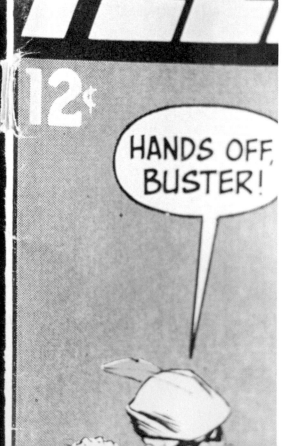

A common defect is the "pulled staple" which occurs when a cover is pulled loose from the stapled spine.

An example of major cover wear in the form of several creases and small tears. Such defects make this comic only in Good condition at best.

An example of waterstain damage on a comic cover.

KING of the CONGO

Comic readers of the past would often write or stamp their names on the cover of a comic to identify it. If the writing on the cover is minor, it can be graded as high as Very Good. If the writing defaces the cover, then the comic can only be Fair or Good at best.

A piece out of cover defect. This missing piece is small enough so that the comic could still be graded as about Good; larger pieces missing would make the book only Fair.

Tape on the inside of a comic, as pictured here, or on the cover of the book is considered a major defect.

A "triple defect." Note the major spine damage and water staining as well as a large cover tear. Such significant defects put this comic in only Fair condition. Notice also that the arrival date (MAR 19) is also stamped on the cover.

An example of a comic in Fair condition. Notice the heavy cover wear and small pieces missing from the front cover. (Tales of Suspense, #12, Marvel Comics).

An example of a comic in Good condition. Notice the moderate amount of spine wear as well as writing on the cover.

An example of a comic in Very Good condition. Although free of any major defects, there is a fair amount of wear on the cover and at the staples. (Daredevil #1, Marvel Comics).

An example of a comic in Fine condition. The book appears clean and sharp and shows some wear along the spine and at the top of the cover. (*Brave and Bold Comics #61*, DC Comics)

An example of a comic in Very Fine condition. The book appears almost new and would be graded as Near Mint except for the "bumped" upper left corner and small flaking on the lower right corner. Note also the signs of staple stress on the top staple. (Batman #65, DC Comics).

An example of a Near Mint to Mint comic. The book is almost perfect, except for "bumped" corners at the spine. Notice too that the cover is very slightly off-centered which would prevent it from being graded as Pristine Mint. (Conan #3, Marvel Comics).

Comic collectors long ago treated their comics casually, and gave no thought to proper storage or preservation of their books.

Today's comic collector stores his comics in specially constructed boxes to preserve and protect them.

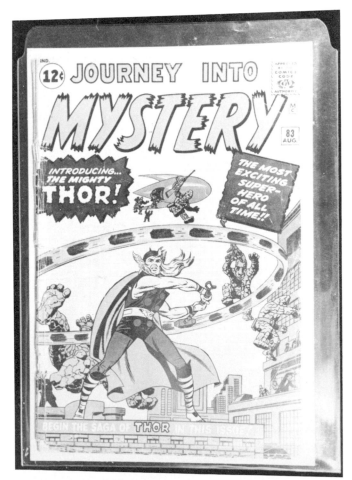

A comic stored in a Mylar bag with an acid-free cardboard backing—the preferred method of preserving valuable comics.

A typical selection of comic collecting accessories at a comic book specialty store: plastic bags, protective cardboard backing, and acid-free storage boxes.

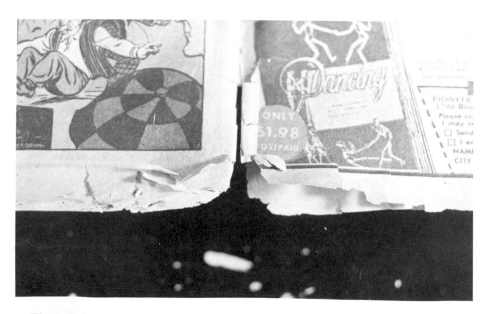

The last days of a comic book. After a comic has become brittle from natural aging and poor storage conditions, it begins to crumble and fall apart. Once a comic has reached this stage, it should be removed from all other books in your collection.

Spine roll is a defect caused by improper storage or reading of a comic. Here are three examples of spine roll: light, medium, and severe.

An example of a valuable comic, ALL WINNERS #1. Besides being the first issue of a Marvel comic from 1941, it also features several of the more popular Marvel comic characters and also contains artwork by Jack Kirby. The combination of all these factors (artist, #1 issue, popular characters, and a widely collected comic company) make this a desirable book.

The comic on the left has the "direct only" distribution box in the bottom corner of the cover. The other comic shows the newsstand UPC box on the cover.

The man who will buy your comic books: the office and stock room of a professional comic dealer.

Collectors should not overlook the many comics which reprint scarce and valuable books. These reprints are an inexpensive way to read and collect older comics. Pictured here is the original Amazing Spiderman #1 which can cost up to $900, and the reprint version of the same comic which can be purchased for under a dollar.

the book's spine. This damage first appears as a thin white line along the edge of the spine. Gradually the spine will start to crack, and minor tears will develop.

- **Cover wear.** Light nicks and creases soon appear along the edge of a comic's cover. Dents and small tears may also occur during the normal reading of a book. Eventually, very small chips may be missing from the cover or spine and some color flaking may develop. In addition, a very small amount of wrinkling may appear on the cover if the book has been exposed to high humidity, and the staples may also have started to rust.

As long as these nicks, tears, creases, chips, and wrinkles are within ⅛ inch to ¼ inch, the defects are considered minor. There may even be a small water stain where a single drop of water touched the comic. All in all, such minor defects are acceptable on a book that is not graded higher than Fine–to–Very Fine condition. Of course, if the book has *many* small nicks, tears, and creases, even if they're less than ¼ inch, then the book must be graded at a lower condition.

Major Wear Defects. Once a comic has developed tears, creases, and nicks larger than a ¼ inch, then the defects are considered to be major and more noteworthy. Here are the major condition defects a comic book may have:

- **Heavy spine wear.** A comic's spine may become "rolled" if it is read with the cover pulled back around the comic or if it is stacked flat in a large pile of comics. Rolled spines may vary from a slight curve to the entire book being pulled off-center. Other spine wear and damage includes separation of the comic at the spine, a major tear at the top or bottom of the spine, and "bumped" or smashed spines at the top or bottom from being stored in a newsstand rack.

- **Major cover wear.** Large creases and folds may appear on the cover. Water stains, discoloration, and tearing of the cover at the staples are other common cover defects.

All these major defects keep a comic from being better than Very Good or Very Good to Fine. If the book has very many such defects, then it can be no better than a Good copy.

Damaged Comics

Once a comic has been damaged, it can be graded only as Fair or Fair to Good or even Poor if the damage is severe. A common mistake is to accept such damages as normal comic wear. While it is true that many older comics will be damaged in some way or the other, that does not mean that these damages can be ignored in the normal grading of a book. Here are the various damages a comic book may have:

- **Tape repairs.** Readers and collectors in the past who didn't know better sometimes used tape to repair a comic or its cover. Often tape was used on the spine to reenforce it. Today's comic collectors know better, and they never use tape to repair a comic.

- **Pieces of chunks out.** A chunk of the cover may be gone, or pieces may be missing from the interior pages of a comic.

- **Water damage and stains.** Large water spots, food stains, ink or paint spills, mildew, grease marks, etc., are considered damages and not defects.

- **Writing.** A very small amount of writing on the cover (such as the arrival date or the owner's name) may be an acceptable defect. Large amounts of scribbling, inking, and coloring on the book's cover or pages make it a damaged copy, however.

- **Holes** punched through the book or chewed by rodents, insects, or other pests are another source of damage in older comics.

- **Loose covers** or coverless books are damaged comics, although the cover may be professionally reattached to repair such damage.

- **Missing pages,** clipped coupons or order blanks, and torn centerfolds also are major damages for a book

Since comics are so easily damaged, a book with only one or two minor damages may be listed and graded as if the damage had not occurred, with the damage noted separately. For example, if a book looks almost brand-new except for a water stain on the back cover, then a collector might describe it as "Fine, with water damage on back cover."

There are many more damages and defects a comic may have. I've seen books ripped completely in half and then retaped. I've found globs of peanut butter and grape jelly along the centerfold of a comic 30 years old, and I've had a book whose back cover had been tortured by multiple cigarette burns. I've seen comic books that have been "smoked" in home fires, warped by flood waters, and run over by a car (the tire tread was still on the back cover).

The Standard Grading Definitions

The grading of a comic must be the same for everyone. If a comic book is graded as Fine, that should mean the same thing to all collectors. In other words, there have to be condition standards in any field of collecting, and comic books are no different.

Most dealers and collectors use the grading standards as outlined in *The Comic Book Price Guide,* edited by Robert M. Overstreet. These are reproduced here, with permission, so that condition standards may become more uniform throughout the hobby.

Pristine Mint (PM): "File copies; absolutely perfect in every way, regardless of age. The cover has full lustre, is crisp, and shows no imperfections of any sort. The cover and all pages are extra white and fresh; the spine is tight, flat, and clean; not even the slightest blemish can be detected around the staples, along spine, at corners or edges. Arrival dates *pencilled* on the cover are acceptable. As comics must be truly perfect to be graded PM, they are obviously extremely scarce even on the newstand. Books prior to 1964 in this grade bring 20 to 50 per cent more."

Mint (M): "Like new or newsstand condition, as above, but with very slight loss of lustre, or a slight off-centered cover, or a minor printing error. Could have pencilled arrival dates, slight color fading, and white to extra white cover and pages. Any defects noticeable would be very minor and attributable to the cutting, folding, and stapling process."

Near Mint (NM): "Almost perfect; tight spine, flat and clean; just enough minor defects of wear noticeable with close inspection to keep it out of the Mint category; i.e., a small flake of color missing at a staple, corner or edge, or slight discoloration on inside cover or pages; near perfect cover gloss retained."

Very Fine (VF): "Slight wear beginning to show; possibly a small wrinkle or crease at staples or where cover has been opened a few times; still clean and flat with most of cover gloss retained."

Fine (FN): "Tight cover with some wear, but still relatively flat, clean and shiny with no subscription crease, writing on cover, yellowed margins or tape repairs. Stress lines around staples and along spine beginning to show; minor color flaking possible at spine, staples, edges or corners."

Very Good (VG): "Obviously a read copy with original printing lustre and gloss almost gone; some discoloration, but not soiled; some signs of wear and minor markings, but none that deface the cover; usually needs slight repair around staples and along spine which could be rolled; cover could have a minor tear or crease where a corner was folded under or a loose centerfold; no chunks missing, tape or brown pages."

Good (G): "An average used copy complete with both covers and no panels missing; slightly soiled or marked with possible creases, minor tears or splits, rolled spine and small color flaking, but perfectly sound and legible. A well-read copy, but perfectly acceptable with no chunks missing, tape or brown pages."

Fair (F): "Very heavily read and soiled, but complete with possibly a small chunk out of the cover; tears needing repairs and multiple folds and wrinkles likely; damaged by the elements, but completely sound and legible."

Poor (P): "Damaged; heavily weathered; soiled; or otherwise unsuited for collection purposes."

Grading: A Step-by-Step Guide

Simply reading the above condition definitions may not mean too much to you yet. Only after you have had practice in grading, buying, and selling comics will you be able to quickly determine a book's condition.

To help you figure out what condition your comic is in, here's a step-by-step series of questions for determining a book's grade.

First, examine your comic book very carefully. Look for any defects as described earlier in this chapter. The major condition categories are listed below, beginning with Poor and working up to Pristine Mint. Within each category is a series of questions. If you answer yes to any question in a category, then the comic is in that condition category. If you answer no to all the questions in one category, then go on to the next test until you answer yes to a question.

Although not *completely* accurate, these test questions will help you refine your grading technique.

The Poor Test

If any of the following defects are present, the comic is only in Poor condition:

1. Is the cover separated, heavily ripped, or missing more than ⅛ of the total cover?

2. Are there any missing pages or cutouts?

3. Is the book brittle or crumbling?

If you answered No to all these questions, then your comic is in at least Fair condition, and you can go to the next series of questions. If you answered yes to any of these questions, then your comic is in Poor condition.

The Fair Test

If any of the following defects are present, the comic is only in Fair condition:

1. Are the interior pages dark brown?

2. Are there any chunks missing from the cover?

3. Are there rusted or broken staples?

4. Are there *many* folds, creases, or wrinkles in the book's cover?

5. Are there *large* rips or tears?

If you answered no to these questions, then your comic has passed the Fair test, and you may go to the next series of questions.

The Good Test

If any of the following defects are present, the comic is only in Good condition:

1. Are there any water marks or other stains on the book?

2. Are there any loose pages or centerfolds?

3. Is there any tape on the book?

4. Is the spine split?

5 Are there any chunks or pieces missing anywhere from the cover?

6. Is there any sign of medium-to-dark browning on the interior pages?

If you answered no to these questions, you may go on to the next condition test.

The Very Good Test

If any of the following defects are present, the comic is only in Very Good condition:

1. Is the cover dull, faded, or generally worn?

2. Are there any tears or chipping on the cover?

3. Is the spine rolled?

4. Are there any markings on the comic (other than arrival dates)?

5. Is there a subscription crease?

6. Are the margins of the inside pages heavily yellowed?

If you answered no to all questions, you may go on to the next test.

The Fine Test

If any of the following defects are present, the comic is only in Fine condition:

1. Are there any creases on the cover?

2. Are the inside pages light yellow or discolored more than an off-white?

3. Are there any creases, wrinkles, or wear along the spine of the comic?

The Very Fine Test

If any of the following defects are present, the comic is only in Very Fine condition:

1. Is there wear or creasing around the staples on the spine?

2. Can you see any small nicks, chips, or any major defect on the front *or* back cover?

3. Are the pages darker than off-white?

4. Has the cover gloss faded?

The Near-Mint Test

If any of the following defects are present, the comic is only in Near-Mint condition:

1. Are there stamped or inked dates on the cover?

2. Are the pages discolored?

3. Are there any small flakes of coloring missing at a staple, corner, or edge?

4. Are there any defects whatsoever except for printing and distribution defects?

The Mint Test

If any of the following defects are present, the comic is in Mint condition. If *none* of these defects are present, the comic is in Pristine Mint condition.

1. Is the cover unsymmetrical?

2. Are the staples off-center?

3. Are the pages less than extrawhite?

4. Does the book appear read in any way?

5. Can you find absolutely anything wrong with the comic?

After a few weeks or months, you will not have to go through such elaborate series of questions or tests. In fact, you'll soon be able to pick up any comic and know its condition within a few seconds.

Like everything else, good grading comes with practice.

How Condition Affects a Comic's Price

"I've got a comic book worth about a thousand dollars," the voice on the phone told me. "You want to buy it?"

"Well, I want to look at it anyway," I replied, and we arranged a meeting.

The man's "thousand-dollar" comic book was a copy of *Wonder Woman #1*. In perfect shape, the comic would probably fetch $900 to $1200. When I saw his copy, I groaned.

The comic's cover had been chewed along the edges by a rat. Worm holes had been eaten through most of the margins of the book, and the rest of the pages were a rich chocolate brown and falling apart as I turned them.

I didn't have the heart to tell the gentleman that his "thousand-dollar find" was worth about $50, tops. Rodents, insects, and Father Time had eaten up the other $950 worth.

The condition of a comic book is the number-one factor in determining its price. But exactly how does condition affect a comic book's worth?

In today's marketplace, a Mint comic book is now worth approximately *six times* as much as a book in only Good Condition. A Fine comic book is worth three times as much as a Good book, while a Fair comic may be worth only one-half or one-third the value of a Good comic.

For example, suppose a comic book is worth $100 in Good condition. Here are the typical values for such a book, based on condition:

Condition	Market Value
Good	$100
Very Good	$200
Fine	$300
Very Fine	$450
Mint	$600

Why is there such a wide difference in prices for the same comic book in different conditions? The answer, in a word, is availability.

Condition and Availability

Comics in nicer shape are worth more because there are far fewer books in the top grades. Most comics in circulation that are read and reread are rarely found in better than Very Good condition. Most such books are usually in Good or Fair condition after several years of reading or improper storage. This is not as true for the more recent comics of the past ten or fifteen years as it is for the older comics from the 1940s through the 1960s. In recent years, many comics have been purchased new off the stands and stored carefully in their original condition. Before the late 1960s, however, new comics were not stored in large quantities.

So there is a good reason for the higher prices on books in top conditions; such books are hard to find, and few collectors want to sell comics in such nice condition. Often collectors will keep their top-condition books in their own collections and sell off the lower-range books.

Alphabet Soup

Dealers and collectors use a wide variety of abbreviations to describe the grades, conditions, and defects of comic books.

The following ad appeared in a national comic collectors' newspaper:

FOR SALE: *Avengers #4* (Captain America revived); ½" crease lower rt. cor.; slight sp. roll; woc; water stain bc; OW VG + /FN. Make cash offer or will trade for early DCs.

Maybe the above description sounds like a foreign language to you, but longtime collectors would immediately know the following information about the condition of the comic offered for sale: There's a small crease on the front cover in the lower right corner, the spine of the comic is slightly rolled, some writing exists on the cover of the book, and there is a water stain on the book's back cover. Otherwise, the comic is in better than very good condition and almost in Fine shape.

Dealers and collectors use two categories of abbreviations to describe the books they have for sale:

1. The overall condition of the book (Good, Fine, Mint, etc.)

2. The various defects and damages the book may have (torn cover, split spine, writing on cover, etc.)

Let's wade through the alphabet soup and examine the information you need to be able to read comic book ads and dealers' catalogs.

Condition Abbreviations

The following abbreviations are often used to describe the general condition of a comic:

P   — Poor condition

FA   — Fair condition

FR   — Fair condition

F   — Fair condition (but usually used to indicate a Fine-condition book)

G   — Good condition

VG   — Very Good condition

F   — Fine condition (*Warning:* Some dealers use this as an abbreviation for Fair comics; ask if you're not sure)

FN   — Another abbreviation for Fine condition; often used to distinguish it from Fair condition

VF   — Very Fine condition (hardly ever used to describe a book as Very Fair)

VFN   — Very Fine condition

NM   — Near-Mint condition

M   — Mint condition

PM   — Pristine Mint condition (used to describe a "perfect" comic)

In addition, the abbreviations *A* and *N* are often used with a condition abbreviation to specify a comic that is Almost Good or Almost Fine or Near Fine, as in these examples:

AVG   — About Very Good (*Warning:* Some dealers use this to describe an average-condition comic, which may or may not be in about Very Good condition.)

AFN   — About Fine condition

NG   — Near good

The *about* and *near* descriptions and abbreviations are used to indicate a comic that is almost, but not quite, the condition given.

Other, less common, condition abbreviations are *E* for either "excellent" or "extremely," as in the abbreviation:

EFN   — Extra or extremely Fine

or just:

E   — To describe a book in Excellent condition, which usually indicates a Fine–to–Very Fine book, depending on the dealer's standards

In addition, collectors and dealers may "split" grades when describing a book's condition. For example, if the comic is better than Very Good condition, but not quite Fine, then it may be listed as: VG/FN, VG–FN, VGF, or VG–F.

Other examples of split grades are:

FRG   — Fair to Good

G/VG   — Good to Very Good

VF/NM   — Very Fine to Near Mint

F–VFN   — Fine to Very Fine

Finally, conditions may be qualified with a plus sign (+) or minus sign (−) to indicate a book that is either slightly better or slightly worse than the condition described. For example, if a book is better than Very Good, but not at all near Fine, then it may be listed as: VG+.

On the other hand, a book may be very close to being in fine condition but may have one or two very minor defects that keep it from that category. In this case, it might be listed as: FN−.

With split grades and plus and minus signs, the condition of a comic can be pinpointed. To help you understand which grade is better than another, let's look at the different grades a comic may have between Very Good and Fine condition, in the order of lowest to highest:

AVG   — About Very Good; the next step above G/VG condition

VG−   — Very Good–minus; not quite VG; usually considered to be slightly better than About Very Good

VG   — Very Good condition

VG+   — Very Good–plus; slightly better than Very Good

VG/FN   — Very Good to Fine; exactly halfway between a book in Very Good condition and one that is in Fine shape

VG+/FN — Very Good–plus to Fine

NFN   — Near Fine; also may be abbreviated as *AFN* for "About Fine."

FN−   — Fine-minus; not quite Fine condition, but very close

FN   —Fine condition (may also be specified as *F*)

Most books do not need to be described in such fine detail; most comics are listed in a major condition grade such as VG or NM, without all the splitting and minor qualifications. Expensive books, however, are often described in such close grading because it can make a real difference in price.

For example, an early issue of *All Star Comics* from the 1940s is worth $300 in good condition and $900 in Fine. In Very Good condition, it would be worth $600. (Remember that a Very Good comic has a value exactly halfway between Good and Fine.) Now let's look at our different grades from Very Good to Fine and see how they affect the price of such a comic:

Condition	Value
AVG	$500
VG –	$550
VG	$600
VG +	$675
VG/FN	$750
VG + /FN	$800
NFN	$850
FN –	$875
FN	$900

As you can see, a split grade can mean $50 or more in the price of a really valuable comic. On the other hand, for a comic worth only $3 or $4, such fine distinctions are rarely needed, since they affect the book's value by an insignificant amount.

Defect Abbreviations

"What condition is your comic in?"

"Not too bad; it's got an RS with a CT; some WRBC and a CFL, but at least there's no POC."

Collectors don't really talk this way, but they often use such abbreviations in ads and lists to describe books they have for sale. Abbreviations save typing and valuable ad space. If you order by mail, you'll need to know what these abbreviated descriptions mean.

Here are the abbreviations used most often to describe a comic book's defects:

BC — Back cover; used as in "stain on BC"

BR — Brown or brittle; some collectors use BRN to denote the browning of comic pages and BRT to indicate that the pages have passed the browning stage and are now turning brittle

C	— Coverless; sometimes abbreviated as CVLS or Cov. Also used as an abbreviation for "cover," such as "water spot on C"
CC	— Coupon cut; indicates that an order blank or coupon in the comic has been cut out. Also sometimes abbreviated as *CPO* for "coupon out" or *CPM* for "coupon missing"
CF	— Centerfold; the center pages of a comic
CFL	— Centerfold loose; indicates that the center page of the comic is no longer attached to the staples
CFO	— Centerfold out; the center pages are missing, and the book is no longer complete. Occasionally listed as *CFM* for "centerfold missing"
CHP	— Chip; very small pieces of cover or page are missing. Chipping is also indicated by the abbreviation *CH*
CL	— Cover loose from staples.
CR	— Crease; used as in "1-inch CR on cover." May also be used to mean "corner," as in "small tear on RT CR"
CS	— Cover stain
CT	— Cover tear, as in "minor CT"
LF	— Left; such as "stain on LF of BC"
MC	— Sometimes used to indicate a condition known as "Marvel chipping." This occurred in the early Marvel comics from the 1960s, which exhibited a tendency to chip all along the right-hand edge of a cover. Some collectors use the term to describe any comic, Marvel or not, that has small chips missing from its cover on the right edge.
OW	— Otherwise, as in "some damage, OW Very Good." Also abbreviated *O/W*
PC	— Piece; as in "small PC missing"
POC	— Piece out of cover

POBC   — Piece out of back cover

RS   — Rolled spine

RT   — Right; as in "RT corner of cover

SC   — Subscription crease; also abbreviated *SF* for subscription fold. Indicates a comic that has been folded in half vertically and sent through the mail

SP   — Spine of book

SS   — Spine split; indicates that the spine of the book is worn and is now splitting along its edge

ST   — Spine tear or spine taped; preferred use is for spine tear. For "spine taped" see "TS" (*Note: ST* may also be used as an abbreviation for "stain," such as "ink ST on back cover")

TC   — Tape on cover; may also be used to mean "torn cover," but the abbreviation *CT* should be used in this case

TS   — Tape on spine; may also be used for a "torn spine," but the abbreviation *ST* should be used in this case

T   — Usually indicates a tear, although it may also stand for "tape"

TP   — Indicates tape repair to comic

TR   — Tear on comic

WD   — Water damage

WS   — Water stain

WOC   — Writing on cover

WBC   — Writing on back cover

WOP   — Writing on inside pages

WP   — Sometimes used to indicate white pages, which means that the inside pages of the book have not begun to yellow or turn brown

YL   — Yellowing; sometimes abbreviated *Y*. Indicates that the interior pages of a comic have turned from white to yellow but have not yet started to brown

You'll also discover that collectors and dealers are very creative people when it comes to inventing new terms and abbreviations to describe a comic's condition. For example, here's one description of a comic book that I puzzled over for days until I finally called the dealer who had it in his list:

Captain Marvel #18, *sm ph on bc, noc, id lw rt cr, ch upp sp, w/tp 2–3 pp, ow tight, complete; orig stp, not rusted, pages sup and abt G.*

You have three minutes to figure out what he's talking about. Give up? Here's his translation:

Captain Marvel #18. *Has small pinholes through back cover and a name written on the front cover. There's some insect damage on the lower-right-hand corner of the book. The upper spine has been chewed, and there are minor tape repairs on two or three pages. Otherwise, the book is complete and solid; not falling apart. It has its original staples with no signs of rust; the pages are supple (that is, they're not turning brittle), and the book would be in about Good Condition.*

Fortunately, most comic book descriptions are not so cryptic as this one, and oftentimes an advertiser will provide his own translation key somewhere in the ad if he uses such common abbreviations.

Practical Tips for Determining a Comic's Condition

The hardest part about grading a comic book is being fair and objective. It's easy to ignore defects in a book that you are offering for sale, and it's also tempting to downgrade a book that you are considering buying.

In fact, experienced collectors often joke that a comic book really has two conditions: one that you buy at and another that you sell at. It's always a mystery how a comic that you purchased in Very Good condition a few years ago suddenly has turned into a Fine book when it's time to sell it.

Overgrading comics may simply mark you as inexperienced; at worst, it may brand you as dishonest. Here are some hints to help you develop an objective eye when grading comics:

1. Before you grade a book, remove it from its protective plastic or Mylar bag. A book in a bag will always look about a half grade better than it really is.

2. Never grade a book by its cover alone. I have seen beautiful comics with full glossy covers and no signs of any defects. Yet when the comic is opened, the pages may be dark yellow or even brown and brittle. One comic was sold to me as Fine, and so it seemed to be until you looked inside. Every panel in the book had been outlined in red ink. Evidently the dealer who had the comic never opened the book before he graded it.

3. Before you call a book Mint or Near Mint, compare it to a comic that has just been printed. Look at the comic's back cover as well. The back cover of a book will often show more fingerprints, smudges, and other signs of handling than the brightly colored front cover. If you find any signs of wear, resist grading the book Mint or almost Mint.

4. The grade of a comic book has absolutely nothing to do with its age. A Mint comic book published 40 years ago should look the same as a Mint comic published 40 days ago. So many amateurs often will say about an old comic book, "But it is in Fine condition, considering how old it is." While people may be considered to be in fine shape for their age, comic books must remain ageless when it comes to grading. Ignore the age, ignore the scarcity of the comic, and ignore how desirable the book may otherwise be when you sit down to grade it.

4. Grade twice. After you have assigned a comic a grade, write it down and store the book away for at least a few days and preferably for a few weeks or even a few months or a year. Now go back and grade the book again *before* you look at the first condition you assigned it. If you grade the book the same way twice, you're probably on target. If you discover that you graded the book higher either the first or second time, then always assign the book the *lower* grade.

6. When in doubt, undergrade. No one will ever complain if you sell a book a little better than as you describe it. Many reputable dealers will often assign a book about a half grade less than it really may be just to allow for some collectors' stricter grading standards. It's a good

practice—just don't intentionally undergrade so low that you lower the value of the book greatly.

For the beginning collector, grading a comic may seem difficult or intimidating. However, with practice you'll quickly become an expert. After a few months of collecting, you'll be able to pick up any comic and determine its approximate condition within ten seconds.

Just be *fair;* grade *good,* and you'll do *fine.*

TAKING CARE OF
YOUR COLLECTION

Long ago, before comic book stores and price guides and high prices for back-issue books, comic collectors treated their collections casually. They were likely to have their comic books stashed under their beds or piled into a heap in a spare closet.

When I was a young collector, 25 years ago, the favorite way to store comic books was in a large box in your bedroom closet. I would always grab comics from the bottom of the box, read them at lunch or bedtime, and toss them back onto the top of the stack. After a few weeks, the comics on top of the pile would migrate back down to the bottom, and I'd start again, reading my entire collection every few months, over and over.

I never worried about taking care of my comics; I just read them until the covers fell off and the center pages became ragged.

Today's collectors are now likely to spend as much time and money protecting and preserving their comics as they do finding and reading them. And for good reason, too. A valuable comic book, poorly treated, can become worthless overnight—or even in a few seconds.

One evening I was invited over to view a collector's recently acquired copy of *Batman #1*. He had paid several thousand dollars for it, and he wanted to show it off. There the book was, lying on his dining-room table.

He picked the comic up from the table and held it in his hands as he showed me the cover (he didn't let me hold it since my hands might be dirty). He carefully laid the book back down on the table. Then he screamed.

The back cover of the book was curling up! He had laid it down in a spot where a cold glass of water had sat a few minutes before, and it now was rapidly soaking up a wet circle of water left by the glass. *Batman #1* now had a nice, wet ring on its back cover and was worth a few hundred dollars less. I quietly left a grown man in tears, crying over his comic book.

The moral is this: A valuable comic book has to be treated very carefully. It must be protected at all times. If my friend had kept his book in a plastic bag, then he would have avoided the accidental water damage.

Comic books are valuable because they are so easily damaged. Few survive the onslaught of humidity, heat, careless storage, and the peanut-buttered fingers of casual readers. A creased cover, a torn page, or a brittle spine can decrease the worth of a valuable book by hundreds of dollars.

The days of throwing your comics into a shoe box are gone. If you want to collect, you got to protect.

Here are the best (and worst) places to store your comic book collection.

The Best Place for Your Comics

The best storage conditions for comic books, or any paper items, are:

1. An average humidity of 40 percent. Too much moisture in the air will cause paper decay, curling of covers, and yellowing. Too little moisture, while not as destructive as too much, will also cause the pages of a book to become brittle and will hasten spine deterioration. If you live in a humid climate, keep the books in an air-conditioned and dehumidified room. If you live in the arid Southwest or in an over-heated, dry house, then you may need to use a humidifier in your collection room. Ideally, comics should remain in a constant 40–50-percent humidity range.

2. Dark. Sunlight can yellow and decay fragile comic book paper. Fluorescent light is even worse. Comic books displayed under fluorescent lights decompose and lose color rapidly. Comic book stores especially should be careful about displaying and hanging their valuable comics where sunlight or fluorescent light can get to them.

3. Cool. Comics like it cold. Heat accelerates the decomposition process and makes books brown and brittle. In fact, if it weren't for the humidity, a refrigerator or freezer would be a good place to store comics. Of course, the typical comic collector has so many comics that a refrigerator would soon be filled with nothing but books with no room for food. That's no problem for the really serious fan, however, who would rather read comics than eat, anyway.

   Seriously, a nice cool room is ideal for storing your comics. Look at the chart to see how high temperatures can quickly cause a comic to deteriorate.

An example of a good storage location for your collection that meets most of the above conditions is a spare closet in a guest bedroom that is not overheated in the winter. Closets are dark, maintain a relatively constant humidity, and are generally cooler than the rest of the house.

If you're lucky enough to have an extra room, you might use it only for your collection. This way you can control the environment by keeping the curtains drawn to keep out light and heat, maintaining a constant temperature and humidity, and keeping your books away from injury and day-to-day wear.

The Worst Places to Store Your Comic Collection

Some of the worst places to store comics are often just where they end up, such as attics, basements, and garages and other outbuildings.

Never store your comics in an attic, garage, or unattended building outside the house. For some reason, attics and basements always end up as the storage place for unwanted or overly large collections. The high heat, wide range of temperatures and humidity, insects, and other unseen dangers of these places are deadly to comics.

I've been offered many collections for sale that had been stashed in the garage or up in the attic. These books are almost always browned on the inside, with heavily yellowed covers. They also have water damage from high humidity, and the heat has accelerated the decomposition process. Putting your comic collection in the attic or basement is like parking your car underwater. You'll be unpleasantly surprised when you finally retrieve it to sell.

Ways to Preserve Your Comic Books

So now maybe you have a place to keep your collection, perhaps in a nice empty closet or extra bedroom. What can you do to protect the individual comics?

The comic book was not made to last for years. Most people bought them, read them, saved them for a few months, and then threw them away. Consequently, the books were printed on cheap paper such as ground-wood or sulfite-chemical pulp. The cheap paper that comics are printed on has residual acids left in the paper during manufacture. These acids eat away at the comic book and make it brittle and brown. Proper storage can slow down this acidifying process and preserve your books for years longer than they were meant to last.

Careful handling and care when reading comics can also add years to their life. Pages and covers should never be folded back, as this damages the spine.

Here are some methods that collectors use to keep their comic books in top condition.

Plastic Bags

Plastic bags are the cheapest and most common way of storing comic books. The book is placed inside one or two bags, and the top of the bag is folded and perhaps taped, sealing the book inside. A bag can protect your book from moisture, insects, and dirty hands. Besides, they're cheap. You can bag your entire collection for about 2 cents per comic.

The drawback is that plastic bags will decompose, yellow, and eventually give off vapors that can harm the comic book. Books that have been in plastic bags for three years or more may develop a slightly slick and sticky feel as the plasticizers in the bag attack the cover and interior of the book. Plastic bags are unstable, especially if they are exposed to any type of heat, such as in an attic or non-air-conditioned room in the summer.

For short-term storage, such as in a comic book store, at a convention, or for a couple of years in your house, plastic bags are an economical way to protect your comics. But there is a better way.

Mylar Bags

Mylar is a type of "superplastic." It's made to last for hundreds of years without breaking down like ordinary plastic. Mylar gives off almost no vapors that can harm your comics. In fact, Mylar is used by the Library of Congress and other institutions to protect irreplaceable documents.

Mylar comic book bags have been on the market since the late 1970s. Some of the bags are so thick that you can put a comic inside the bag and it will stand up straight on your book shelf without bending.

But Mylar bags are expensive. You'll spend at least 10–50 cents per bag. That may not sound like much, but if you have a collection of only 2,000 books, you could spend a thousand dollars just for the bags!

What most collectors do is to bag up only books worth $5, $10, or more in Mylar, and use the regular plastic bags for their cheaper comics. A good rule of thumb is that you shouldn't spend more than 10–15 percent of your collection's worth to preserve it. Some collectors go overboard. I've seen many comics in Mylar bags that were worth less than the bags themselves.

Deacidification

While plastic and Mylar bags can protect your comics from moisture, sticky fingers, hungry bugs, and other outside attacks, the greatest enemy of your comic books lies within.

As mentioned earlier, comics have traditionally been printed on cheap paper that yellows, browns, and becomes brittle after several years. The pages of a comic are impregnated with acidic fibers. This acid is what makes the book eventually fall apart.

You can deacidify comic books, which will increase their lifespan. Deacidification, however, is a messy and difficult process that is also expensive. If you have a book worth several hundred dollars, however, you may wish to pay a professional to deacidify the comic.

There are also home kits that allow do-it-yourself deacidification. These kits generally involve spraying each page of a comic book with special chemicals, or even disassembling the comic and dipping the book into a tray of alkali solutions. There are also deacidification sheets that can be placed in the middle of a comic for a few days and then removed which offer some protection.

Generally, however, such methods give less than satisfactory results. In some cases, the deacidification process actually yellows the pages of a book and gives them an unpleasant smell. If you have a comic that is valuable enough to be deacidified, you should probably let an expert do it for a reasonable fee.

You can, however, buy a very useful kit that will allow you to test the acidity of your comics. This involves touching the page of a comic with a chemical roll-on stick which will leave a very small dot on the margin. The resulting color of the dot can tell you just how acidic your book is and whether it is in need of deacidification.

Encapsulation and Lamination

Comic books may also be encapsulated in an extra thick Mylar bag. The book is placed inside the bag and then hermetically sealed to lock out all moisture and corrosive elements. Of course, to read a comic that has been encapsulated, you must cut the bag open and then have it resealed again. This isn't much of a problem because very valuable comics may only be read infrequently or not at all.

An advanced form of encapsulation is not only to seal the comic in an indestructible bag, but also to remove all oxygen from the bag and replace it with an inert gas like nitrogen or helium. Oxygen speeds up the aging process of a comic. If the comic can be encapsulated in an oxygen-free environment, then acid deterioration is slowed down.

Encapsulated comics have been estimated to last seven times longer than a comic not so treated, and it is a relatively cheap way of preservation.

Lamination is a process whereby brittle pages of a comic are sprayed with a strengthening solution to prevent further crumbling. This process makes the pages stiffer, heavier, and somewhat shiny. Lamination should probably only be done when the comic has reached a stage of brittleness so that other methods such as deacidification or encapsulation are no longer enough. To allow handling, each laminated comic page is actually encased in plastic, which may or may not affect its value as an investment item.

To Box or Not to Box

Okay, you've got your comics bagged in plastic or Mylar, and maybe you've even had a few of them deacidified. Where do you put them now?

Most collectors will still find a box to stack their comics in. Be careful. If you stack your comics too high in a box, you risk curling the spines, which can decrease the books' value. But the real danger of using boxes to store your comics is that the cardboard the boxes are made from is also highly acidic, even more so than the comics themselves. The boxes give off invisible acid vapors that age your comics and cause them to deteriorate. For long-term storage, you really shouldn't put your comics in ordinary cardboard boxes.

You can, however, buy special boxes from comic book shops and through the mail that are made from nonacidic cardboard. These boxes have been buffered with alkalis that prevent acid migration from the box to your comics.

Several dealers offer boxes specifically made to store comics and magazines. Besides offering sturdy protection, these alkali-buffered boxes actually help prolong the life of your comics and can absorb some of the harmful acid vapors given off by the stored comics.

You can also make wooden boxes to store your comics in, and some collectors store their most valuable books in a cedar chest, which offers some insect protection as well. The only danger in using wooden boxes is that wood, too, gives off acidic vapors and also may have chemical residues (in plywood, particularly) that can injure your comics.

Besides alkali-buffered boxes, the next-best type of box to put comics in is a metal filing cabinet or safe-deposit box. Metal boxes and cabinets do not give off any harmful vapors that will age your comics.

Cardboard Sheets

Some collectors also buy nonacidic cardboard sheets to use as backing for their comics. Why? Try to stand a bagged comic upright in a box or on your shelf. Unless it's in a thick Mylar bag, the comic will slip inside the bag and bend. This causes the spine to roll and the book to become creased. Comic book covers alone just aren't sturdy enough to offer support and protection for the comic. The solution is to insert a piece of nonacidic cardboard backing into the bag along with the comic. The cardboard sheet keeps the comic from being bent or rolling and offers additional protection to the spine. The nonacidic backing also absorbs some of the comic's natural acidity and so prolongs its life.

Just make sure that the cardboard backing is indeed buffered with alkalis and is not common cardboard. Knowingly sticking a piece of regular acidic cardboard into a closed bag with a comic is premeditated destruction. Within a few years, the comic touching the ordinary cardboard will be heavily yellowed and almost worthless. Alkali backing boards can be purchased from the same dealers who sell alkali-buffered comic boxes or Mylar bags.

Mylar, alkali cardboard, buffered boxes, plastic bags—you're probably thinking that preserving your collection is getting to be a lot of work. Compared to many other hobbies, however, comic collecting requires very few accessories or tools. You don't even really have to go to all this trouble if you store your comics carefully in a safe and controlled environment.

For example, just last year, a comic book dealer discovered over a hundred Golden Age comic books from 1941 to 1943 in almost-perfect, brand-new condition. The books showed very little sign of aging, yet they had not been in special bags or boxes. How did they survive so well?

The comics had all been stacked only about 20 high, flat, and on a metal shelf inside a cool closet. They were hardly ever read, and they were not exposed to wide changes in temperature or humidity. The pages were crisp, white, and even smelled new. (Don't tell me you never smelled a comic? The odor of an old comic book has sent some collectors into subdued rapture. Be careful, however, when you sniff—you might be accused of always keeping your nose in a book.)

So if you have a cool room in your house that doesn't become overly humid, you can stack your comics in small piles and without the protection of any bags. Just be sure that the books are kept out of direct sunlight and away from insect (or child) damage. This method is actually far less harmful than storing comics in plastic bags and regular cardboard boxes for long periods.

Repairing and Restoring Comic Books

No matter how careful you are in storing your collection in bags, boxes, etc., one of your books may become damaged by accident or through careless handling. And it's also possible that you'll find an older comic that has a major injury, such as a ripped cover or torn page.

It may be tempting to try to fix up a damaged comic, but listen closely: *Do not attempt to repair a valuable comic book.*

Most amateur efforts at comic book repair will lower the value of a book. Even if you don't botch the repair job, it will usually still be obvious that the book was damaged and inexpertly fixed.

There are professionals who can repair comics and other valuable books and documents. If the comic is worth more than $25, it may be worthwhile to pay a professional to repair damages such as a creased or torn cover, ragged spine, rolled cover, or missing pieces. Professionals who make comic book repairs guarantee their work and are often insured should they make a mistake. People who repair and restore comic books usually advertise in collector publications and in the comic book price guides.

If you can't afford to pay a professional to repair a damaged comic, leave it in its unrepaired condition. Someone who later buys the book may wish to have it expertly repaired. If you've already messed it up, it may not be possible to undo the harm you've done.

You can, however, make very minor repairs to a comic book if you are cautious. The easiest repairs for an amateur to make are reattaching a loose cover or centerfold, which happen to be the two most common defects of well-read comics.

To reattach a loose cover, carefully put a very small dab of library glue on the inside of the cover at the two points where the staples were attached. Now lay the cover flat and opened on a table. Set the coverless comic so that the dabs of glue make contact with the two staple points and press firmly.

To reattach a loose centerfold, open the book to its center and very carefully lift up the two staples so that the centerfold may be reinserted onto the staples. A very small amount of library glue may be used if the centerfold has been torn around the staple contact points. Now bend the staples back down and leave the book opened until the glue dries.

You should always indicate that a comic book has been repaired or restored when you offer it for sale. Even when restored by experts, a repaired comic is usually worth about 25 percent less than one in its original, undamaged condition. Most comic book repairs, however, can improve the book's condition (and hence value) from one-half to one full grade. That is, a Very Good comic may be restored to Fine, or a Good comic may be restored to Very Good.

The most worthwhile comics to have professionally repaired are rare ones in Poor or Fair condition. Such a comic can often be restored to a solid Good copy, which is an acceptable condition for a truly hard-to-find issue.

If the comic is a common and inexpensive issue and not a collector's item, then you can use library glue to reattach covers and pages and make minor repairs. For most comic books, however, leave the repairs to the experts. A poorly restored book is worth much less than an unrepaired comic.

Keeping Track of Your Collection

Okay, now you know how to take care of your collection. You've bought bags, boxes, and buffered cardboard sheets. You've carefully stacked your comics in a cool, dark place. But that's only half the job. Protecting your comics is important, but you also have to know which comics you have and which ones you need. You also need a system that will let you organize your books so you can easily find any comic you might want to read or sell.

Organizing a comic collection is actually a lot of fun, and there are many ways of going about arranging your books. Some collectors store their comics alphabetically by title. In one box they may have all the comics that start with *A, B,* or *C.* In another box (or closet!), they may have all their comics that start with *D, E,* or *F.*

Other collectors prefer to arrange their collections by publisher, putting all the Marvel comics in one place and all the DC comics in another place, for example. Then they arrange each publisher's titles alphabetically. Collectors that specialize in comics by specific artists may keep their comics by one artist in one box and those by a different artist in another box. There are even some collectors who arrange their collections by year, putting all the books from 1980 in one spot, the comics from 1981 in another place, and so on.

The most common method is to store all the issues of one title together in numerical order. Some collectors like to start off with the most recent issue of the title stored first, with the rest of the issues arranged in descending order until the #1 issue is last in the stack. This way, they can simply lay the latest issue on top of their title stack and not have to rearrange it each time. Other collectors prefer to put their #1 issues on top and arrange the rest of the title numbers in ascending order, so that the latest issue is at the bottom of the stack or the back of the box.

It really doesn't matter which method you use, just so you do have some sort of consistent system. The important thing is to develop some method of organizing your collection so you can quickly find a comic that you want and also be able to tell if you are missing a certain issue. You don't know the meaning of frustration until you've searched through 8,000 comic books as you look for that one issue that you want to sell. If you collect, you've got to get organized. There's no getting around it.

The most common way to organize a collection is to sort it first by publisher, then arrange each publisher's titles alphabetically. Within each title, the earliest issues may be stored first so you can flip through your comics from front to back in numerical order as you make up your sale lists and want lists.

Did I hear you ask, What's a want list? Well, hold on. You're not a real collector until you have a want list. A want list is simply a list of comic book titles and numbers that you want for your collection. For example, if you're collecting all the issues of Spider-Man, you make up a list of all the numbers you don't yet have. Such a list can be taken with you when you go comic shopping, or you can easily refer to it when you order comics, instead of digging through your collection each time.

For example, here's one Superman collector's want list:

Action Comics 252, 299, 301–312, 325

Superboy 68, 78–99, 101, 102, 108–125

Superman 100, 129–133, 144, 148

Most collectors' want lists are much longer. You should probably list all the comics you hope to be able to buy for the next several years on your master want list. As you get comics on your list, mark them off immediately so you won't accidentally buy them again. You can make up a want list by studying dealers' lists or comic book price guides, which list all the issue numbers of a particular title. From these lists and catalogs, you can find out which titles and issues are available and which ones you still need.

A beginning collector will probably want more comics than he already has. In this case, a have list might be easier to make up. A have list is often much more useful than a want list. On a have list, you write down each comic that is in your collection by title and issue number. You may also want to write down such information as the condition of the book, how much you paid for it, when you bought it, and its current guide-book value.

For example, here's one Marvel collector's have list:

Comic	Number	Condition
Daredevil	38	Fine
Daredevil	133	Very Good
X-Men	94	Near Mint
X-Men	133	Mint

Notice that the condition of each comic is recorded so that the collector may upgrade to a better-condition copy if he so desires. Also, by recording the condition he can figure out how much his collection is worth.

A have list is more valuable than a want list because not only can you tell which comics you need, but you know which comics are already in your collection and their condition. If you also record the current value of each comic on your have list, you can use it for a sale list if you decide to get rid of your collection, or simply for insurance or inventory purposes.

No matter if you use a want list or a have list, you do need some sort of inventory so you'll know what comics you have in your collection and which ones you still need. Without such a list, you may buy unwanted duplicates or not realize that you need a particular issue.

Some collectors use a computer to make up their inventories. Others write on index cards or make up a special notebook to record their comics. A few collectors can keep all that information juggled in their heads, but for safety's sake you're better off with a written inventory of your collection. Let's look at the different ways you can keep track of your collection.

Computers and Comics

You can buy programs for your home computer that are just for keeping track of comic collections. These programs are often written by other collectors, and they allow you to keep an up-to-date inventory of your collection and its worth. If you have a computer, you should definitely use it to keep track of all your books. There are many programs that you can adapt for your own use that will work well, and it's actually pretty simple to write your own comic inventory program on most home computers.

Here's a sample inventory from one such program:

COMIC BOOK INVENTORY

COMIC NAME	ARTIST	#	DATE	QUAN	COST	MYCOST	RESALE	COND
ACTION	SWAN	500	10/79	1	1.00	.75	1.50	NM
ALPHA FLIGHT	BYRNE	1	08/83	60	1.00	44.90	120.00	M
AMAZ SPID	ROMITA	283	03/83	32	0.60	11.57	18.20	M
AMER FLAGG	CHAYKIN	1	03/83	51	1.00	33.70	76.50	M
CAM 3000	BOLLAND	1	12/82	5	1.00	5.00	25.00	M

Notice that the program allows you not only to record the title, number, and condition of a book in your collection, but also to keep track of such information as artist, date of purchase, original cover cost, the price you paid (MYCOST), and its retail or resale worth (RESALE).

Listen to what else you can do with computers and comics:

"I started collecting comics about three years ago, and for two years I kept track of my collection by hand with index cards and checklists," says Jim, an engineer and comic collector from Knoxville, Tennessee.

"Then one day at work I started talking to a friend of mine who is a computer programmer. We decided that it would be easy to write a program for comic collectors to help them keep up with their collection and to track their investment."

The comic book inventory program records each comic in your collection by name, issue number, condition, and value. In addition, you can enter such information as original cover price, how much you paid for the book, how many copies you own, and comments about each issue (such as artist, publisher, and so on). After you've entered the information for each comic in your collection, then you have a total inventory and a complete record of all your comics.

"I use the program to generate want lists, price lists, indexes, and to track my investments," says Jim. "One main use of the program is to keep an up-to-date inventory of all my comics for insurance purposes. Every six months, I'll run off a copy of my collection inventory and send it to my insurance agent. I was surprised to find out that most collectors do not insure their comics. I think the reason they don't is that it's a lot of work to update and list your collection by hand. The computer takes all the work out of it."

Besides using the computer program to keep a current inventory and to monitor the worth of his collection, Jim also finds it helpful in keeping up with which artists have done what books, and so forth.

"The program has a search routine which is very helpful. For instance, if I want to find out how many comics I have with artwork by Frank Miller, I just type in *Miller* in the appropriate entry field, and the computer will give me a list of all the comics that have Frank Miller art. I can also be very specific, and ask the computer to tell me how much the comics with Miller artwork have increased in value. Then I can ask it for the percentage price increase and compare it to other comic issues to see if my money is being well spent."

With a good computer program to manage your collection, you can list your entire collection and have it sorted alphabetically by comic book name. Then you can print another listing of your entire collection sorted by artist. You'd know immediately which books in your collection have artwork by Neal Adams or Carl Barks. Then you can tell the computer to print out your collection by issue date, so you can have a listing of your comics from the oldest to the newest. You can even print a list of your collection by value so that you can have a record of all your books from the most expensive to the cheapest.

Besides keeping an inventory of your collection, you can also use the computer to track your investments and to help you make a profit.

"I'm primarily an investor," says Jim. "I do read some for pleasure and also just to keep up with the market. I got into collecting, however, mostly out of curiosity. I started buying #1 issues off the newsstands, and then I discovered a local dealer who sold back issues. I bought my first price guide and started looking at the numbers and prices of comics and the rate of price increases. Being an engineer, I started to analyze some of the returns, the compounded appreciation rate per year, and so on. I was astounded at the money, at least on paper, that could be made from comics."

The computer program allows Jim to track his profits and see which comics he should be buying and which ones should be sold. "I watch the percentage increase per year of each comic very carefully, and my program makes it very easy to see which books are moving up in value and which ones aren't."

A computer program can also tell you which comic may be a good buy and which one probably won't make you any money. "Take *X-Men 94*, for example. It guides at $90 or so, but according to my calculations, there's an effective increase in value of only 5 percent per year now. That's too conservative a profit in a field like comic collecting, where most of the top books will get you a 100–200-percent return. A good program will help you track the percentage increase in value for a book instead of just its current price."

Jim has been into collecting for only three years, but he sees computers as a big help in giving the beginner an edge in the investment field. "I've used my program to determine what the top ten comics are, based on investment indicators. Many of the ones that I picked up on have now increased at about 150 percent per year in value. What I don't know yet, having done this for only three years, is what the realities are in the marketplace, how much profit I will really make after I sell them."

Jim also uses the program to track his collection's worth from year to year. "When a new guide comes out, I'll print out my entire collection inventory with their old prices, then have the computer total the prices for me. Next I'll go through and change the values in my collection inventory to match the new guide prices. After that, I have the computer update and print out a new list with the total values. Then, bang, right off the bat I can see how much my collection has increased in worth over the last six months."

Jim currently has over 5,000 comics inventoried with his program, and he updates his computer data base about every month or so. He can analyze his collection for a number of factors, and not all of them relate to investments. For example, a collection-management program can show you which comics you may still need and which of these are increasing in price the fastest. This would help you buy a book before it became even more expensive next year.

If you have a home computer, you should computerize your own collection. Besides Jim's program, there are several other software packages on the market that collectors can adapt for their own use. A computer program can help you manage your collection as well as track your investment, provide a ready list for insurance purposes, and generate want lists and indexes.

Keeping Track by Pencil and Paper

Of course, you don't have to have a computer to keep track of your collection. A pencil and a sheet of paper are really all you need. Let's look at some of the old-fashioned ways you can manage your collection.

Index Cards. For each comic title you collect, take an index card and write the title at the top. Now write all the numbers of that title that you wish to collect. If you're going to try for a complete set, then list all the numbers currently published, as in this example:

The Amazing Spider-Man				
		11	18	25
		12	19	26
1	6	13	20	27
2	7	14	21	28
3	8	15	22	29
4	9	16	23	30
5	10	17	24	31

As you find the issues you need, record the condition of each book by its number. In our example, suppose the collector purchased *Spider-Man* #7 in Very Good condition, #16 in Fine condition, and #30 in Near-Mint condition. He would record his new purchases on the index card like this:

The Amazing Spider-Man				
		11	18	25
		12	19	26
1	6	13	20	27
2	7 VG	14	21	28
3	8	15	22	29
4	9	16 FN	23	30 NM
5	10	17	24	31

You could also record the price paid for the book along with the condition on the card. You could then make up a card for each title you collect and file them all in an index card box.

Notebooks. Besides index cards, many collectors use a loose-leaf note-book to keep track of their collections. They devote each page to a specific title and then list all the numbers of the title that they want to collect. As they find a number they need, they record it in the notebook. Pages can be inserted and removed as you add and subtract titles from your collection. It's a good idea to get a small notebook for this purpose so you can take it with you easily on your comic book buying expeditions.

Most collectors also make up a single page want list from their index cards, computer printouts, or notebook. This way they have a complete record of their collection in one place and also have a convenient list that they can carry with them when they go shopping for comics.

I used to laugh at collectors that kept their comic book want lists in their billfolds or purses, and I made jokes about them being "card-carry-ing comic collectors." But no more. Last summer I chanced upon an out-of-the-way comic shop while on vacation. They had hundreds of inex-pensive comics, but I couldn't remember which ones I needed. Now I keep a copy of my want list in the car's glove compartment, along with automobile insurance papers, a copy of the car title, and other essential documents.

I mean, if you're going to collect comics, you might as well be serious about it, right?

WHAT MAKES A COMIC BOOK VALUABLE?

You can pay $1 for a comic book 25 years old, and you can sell a one-year-old comic for $25. If there's one thing that's hard for the beginning collector to understand, it's this: The age of a comic book has very little to do with its value.

You may read about comics from the 1940s selling for hundreds and thousands of dollars, but the majority of money being spent and made is for comics that are usually less than ten years old. Just because a comic book is 20 or 30 years old does not mean that it is valuable.

In fact, not that many comics are valuable. You can still buy the majority of all comics published for less than $20 each—and that includes issues that were published 30–40 years ago. Since 1938, about 17,000 comic titles have been published. Out of all those, probably fewer than 300 titles attract serious collector interest. So you can see that there are many comics, both old and new, that simply are not valuable. No one collects them, few want them, and it doesn't matter if they were published yesterday or 30 years ago.

But there are valuable comics—thousands of them—and you can learn to recognize what makes one comic worth a lot of money while another sells for less than a dollar.

What makes a comic book valuable? Generally, one or more of these factors:

1. Popularity of the artist who drew the comic

2. Popularity of the character or the title

3. Historical significance of the book

4. Popularity of the comic company that published the book

5. Condition

6. Supply and demand

In some cases, even one of the above factors can make a comic book valuable. For example, the most valuable comic book in the world recently sold for $38,000. It had work by a relatively popular artist (Bill Everett) and featured two classic comic heroes, the Human Torch and the Submariner. More important, it was the first issue published by Marvel Comics, from 1939, and it was in perfect condition.

Let's look in more detail at the qualities that make a comic book valuable.

Popularity of the Artist

A good comic book artist can make a thousand dollars' difference—literally. Back in 1952, a comic book called *Thun'da* was published for six issues. You can still get most of these issues for around ten dollars, except for one: It sells for almost a thousand dollars! What's the difference? The thousand-dollar book was drawn by Frank Frazetta, perhaps the most collectible artist; the others were not.

No other single factor can make a comic book as valuable as the artist who draws the book. Collectors often specialize in collecting books by certain artists. The more well known and liked an artist is, the more valuable the book is likely to be.

Who are the popular comic book artists that can make a book valuable? The list can change monthly due to the popularity of new artists arriving on the scene as well as the changing tastes of the collectors. There are, however, recognized great comic book artists whose works have always been respected and collected.

We've divided the more popular comic book artists into three groups, and while a certain amount of personal opinion is always involved, the following artists are in demand by the collectors.

The Major Artists

These are the top collected artists in the comic book field. Their work has been around for years; they are well respected. They have usually been publishing since the 1940s or 1950s, although a few did not start until the 1960s. Almost any comic with artwork by one of these ten major artists has significant collector value:

Neal Adams
Carl Barks
Reed Crandall
Will Eisner
Frank Frazetta
Walt Kelly

Jack Kirby
Al Williamson
Basil Wolverton
Wally Wood

The Notable Artists

The next group of artists are also highly collected and respected in the comic book field. They, too, have generally been drawing comics since the 1940s and 1950s, although there are a few on this list who didn't start working in comics until the 1960s or early 1970s. Any comic with artwork by one of the following artists is usually of significant interest and value to at least a select group of collectors and investors:

Murphy Anderson	Carmine Infantino
Matt Baker	Graham Ingels
John Buscema	Gil Kane
Sid Check	Joe Kubert
Gene Colan	Harvey Kurtzman
Jack Cole	Russ Manning
L. B. Cole	Joe Orlando
Rich Corben	Bob Powell
Johnny Craig	John Severin
Jack Davis	Barry Smith
Jay Disbrow	John Stanley
Steve Ditko	Jim Starlin
Bill Elder	Jim Steranko
George Evans	Curt Swan
Bill Everett	Alex Toth
Lou Fine	Berni Wrightson
Russ Heath	

Other noteworthy artists, such as Hal Foster, Alex Raymond, Milt Caniff, and others were not listed because they are primarily comic-*strip* artists, and their work appeared only as reprints in the comic books. Nevertheless, books with strip reprints by the classic newspaper comic artists have a respectable collector demand.

The New Artists

There is a third group of artists whose work can make a comic valuable. They are called the new artists because they have done most of their work in only the last five to ten years. Nevertheless, they may be in more demand than the older, established artists because of their popularity with the current generation of readers.

The new-artist list will change more quickly than the other two because new talent appears every year. Names may be dropped or added, but currently these are some of the most popular new comic book artists whose work can make a book valuable:

Terry Austin	Bob Layton
Brian Bolland	Bob McLeod
John Byrne	Frank Miller
Howard Chaykin	Jerry Ordway
Dave Cockrum	George Perez
Keith Giffen	Marshall Rogers
Michael Golden	Bill Sienkiewicz
Butch Guice	Walt Simonson
Paul Gulacy	Paul Smith
Klaus Janson	Timothy Truman

Keep in mind that this list of new artists changes almost monthly. Some of the artists on this list may already have left the comic book field by the time you read this, while new stars appear almost every month. If you don't see your favorite listed above, it does not mean that he is not a significant talent.

An interesting trend in comic collecting is the growing importance of the artist (and occasionally the writer) in determining the popularity (and hence value) of a comic. In the early days of comic collecting, it was the comic character or title that often determined the popularity of the book. Nowadays, it's the artist that will "sell" the book as much as the character that appears in the comic. And that brings us to the second factor that can make a comic valuable.

Popularity of the Character or Comic Title

Besides collecting by artists, collectors also like to get every issue of a comic that features a well-liked character. Often this means collecting all issues of a certain title as well, such as *Action Comics* that feature Superman or *Whiz Comics* that have Captain Marvel. There are indeed popular characters and desirable titles in the comic field.

Among the ten most valuable comic books in the world, Superman appears in two, Batman appears in two, Captain Marvel in two, and Captain America in two. Here's a list of popular characters who have appeared in the most valuable comic books:

Superman
Batman
Captain America
Captain Marvel
Donald Duck
Human Torch
Dick Tracy
Mickey Mouse
Submariner
Wonder Woman
Superboy
Fantastic Four
Spider-Man

There are dozens and dozens of other well-known characters that can make a book valuable. In the current comics, characters can rocket to popularity in a few months. Among the newer characters who are enjoying popularity are the X-Men, the Teen Titans, and Daredevil. Tastes change quickly with these heroes, however, and often simply a change of artist can make or break a new character.

Generally, you are safe in assuming that a character or title that has been published for 20 years or longer is a collector's mainstay and should always prove to be quite collectible.

Besides a good artist and a solid title or character, another important factor in the value of a comic is the actual content of the book—the story line, the subject treatment, the appearances of special characters, or even the number of the issue. This quality is called:

The Historical Significance of the Book

Everyone knows that the first issue of a title is usually the most valuable. That is because #1 issues have a "historical" importance. They usually contain the origin or first appearance of a character. Consequently, these issues bring a significantly higher price than other numbers of the same title.

So what makes a comic book significant and gives it that added collector's appeal?

- All first issues. The first issue of almost any comic book is worth something because there are collectors who want the #1 issue of all titles, regardless of content or artist. In a related development, some collectors also want the #100 issue of any comic title, so issues numbered 100 are also desirable (but not nearly as much as a first issue).

- Origin and debut issues. The first appearance of a popular comic book character is sought out by collectors. This is not always the first issue of a title; for instance, Batman first appeared in *Detective Comics #27,* which is four times as valuable as *Detective Comics #1.*

- Last issues and final appearances. Occasionally, the last issue of a comic is valuable simply because it may have received low distribution or received poor sales.

More recently, however, the trend has been to kill certain popular characters in a comic. So instead of having an "origin" issue, there is a "demise" or "death" issue.

For example, Spider-Man's girlfriend, Gwen Stacy, was killed in issue #121 of Spider-Man, and it is six times as valuable as the previous issue, #120. Although morbid, death issues are usually valuable, depending on the popularity of the character that is killed.

- Cameo and crossover appearances. A crossover or guest appearance is when a popular character from another comic book appears in an issue of another title. Perhaps the most famous such crossover appearance occurred in *Superman #76* in 1952 when Batman costarred with Superman. In this issue, the two famous heroes discovered each other's secret identities. This particular crossover appearance makes this book worth three to four times as much as other issues from the same year.

Appearances by actual people in a comic book can also increase its value. The most valuable appearances are those by the Beatles from some of the comic book stories of the 1960s. Not only comic collectors, but fans of the Beatles seek out these issues. Other such famous people who have appeared in comics and may increase their value are Elvis Presley, John Kennedy, and even Marilyn Monroe.

- Subject treatment. The story of a comic or the manner in which a certain subject is covered can make the book more collectible. For example, some collectors look for comics that are full of propaganda or patriotism, such as the comics from World War II. The treatment of blacks in comics is another area of collecting interest, and some collectors hunt down such comic titles as *All-Negro Comics* and *Negro Romances* that were published in the early 1950s.

Also in the 1950s were comics that were full of violence and suggestive sex scenes. Incidents of bondage, torture, rape, and so on were depicted in these comics, and they are sought out by historians of comic books. Comics dealing with nuclear war, drug abuse, and other controversial areas may also be valuable because of their interesting treatments of such subjects.

In general, this may be the most difficult quality to judge, because collector interest in these subject areas may change quickly. With a careful reading of the comic's contents, however, you may discover that you have a book that is of interest to the specialized collector.

Popularity of the Comic Book Company

There have been hundreds of comic book publishing companies. Many folded during the 1950s, but a half dozen or so have been actively publishing for the last 40 years. Many collectors have a preference for the works of one comic company over another one, and some fans attempt to collect almost every comic published by a particular company.

Historically, the greatest collector interest has been in the books published by Marvel Comics. Marvel collectors are really responsible for the big boom in the comic-collecting field, and the sales of Marvel comic books alone account for more than half of all collector activity.

DC Comics, another major publisher, has usually enjoyed second-best status in the collecting field. Although DC has published more books at a more consistent level of quality than Marvel has, fans seem to prefer Marvel comics. Of course, this trend may change, but it has held for the last 20 years or so.

Rarely, however, does a specific comic company make a book instantly valuable. The exception to this was the EC comic company of the early 1950s. The EC comics were so uniformly outstanding, featuring the best art and stories of their time, that almost any book from this company could be considered valuable.

In general, collectors have concentrated most of their efforts among three or four major comic publishers. Among the top 50 most valuable comic book titles of all time, DC Comics published sixteen, Marvel published nine, Dell published five, and the rest are distributed among seven other publishers who are now out of business. Among the top ten most valuable comic titles of recent years, Marvel has published seven and DC three.

Of course there are exceptions, but as a general rule the safe investor should probably concentrate on the books published by DC and Marvel Comics. These two companies have captured almost 100 percent of the current collector's market, and they are still generating a lot of strong interest among today's readers. Titles and comic companies that stopped publishing ten, twenty, or thirty years ago do have an appeal for the advanced collector, but any dealer will tell you that the backbone of his business is among Marvel and DC collectors.

Condition of Comic Books and Their Value

Condition alone cannot make a comic book valuable. There are about as many collectors who want a mint copy of *Space Mouse #8* as those that want a good copy—about zero. Most collectors, however, do want the comics they collect, whatever they might be, in as nice a shape as possible.

Excellent-condition books that are collectible are worth more than poorer-condition books. That's a fact of collecting lore. Low-grade and heavily worn or read comics are difficult to sell—even if they are "valuable" books.

Desirable comic books that are almost like new (Mint or Near Mint) are always easy to sell to collectors. The most valuable books are in these top conditions. An already valuable comic in excellent shape can command a premium price. A damaged book, even if it would otherwise be valuable, can bring only a fraction of its potential worth.

Supply and Demand

The more collectors that want a comic and the fewer copies that are available, the faster the price of the comic will rise. That seems simple enough except for one problem: Nobody really knows how many issues of a particular comic are available in the collector's market.

We do know, for the most part, about how many copies of a comic are originally issued by the publisher, but there is no way of figuring out how many make it into the hands of collectors and how many simply disappear.

In the 1940s, a publisher might put out 300,000–400,000 copies of each comic book they issued. The really popular titles sold up to 1 million or more copies each month, and for awhile, the popular *Walt Disney Comics and Stories* had a monthly circulation that approached 2 million copies.

Starting in the early 1950s, print runs were decreased for comic books. By the late 1960s, the average comic book had a circulation of 150,000–200,000 copies. Comic book circulation has decreased since that time, and now most current comic books are published in quantities of about 100,000–125,000.

Of course, out of all those comics, most were lost, destroyed, or discarded within the first year. Quite simply, there is no way that the supply of any comic book can be accurately known.

We do know from experience, however, that certain comics seem to turn up rarely. They are difficult to find, and hence are called "scarce" or "rare." The definitions of scarce, rare, and very rare comics are as follows:

Scarce   20–100 copies estimated to exist

Rare   10–20 copies estimated to exist

Very Rare 1–10 copies estimated to exist

Simply because a comic is scarce or rare, however, does not mean that it is extremely valuable. After all, if no one wants a comic book, it doesn't matter if one or a thousand copies exist.

Collector demand is really what determines the value of any comic book. As demand increases for a particular comic, its price goes up. When the price of a comic reaches a certain point, other collectors decide that it's time to sell the copies that they have in their own collections. When these comics enter the marketplace, the current supply of that book increases. If enough comics are put into circulation, then the price could even fall if the demand remains steady or decreases.

The price of any collectible or commodity is dictated by the law of supply and demand. In the comic book field, however, it is impossible to gauge the available supply, and collector demand is a subjective, perceived quality that is also difficult to measure.

Collector demand may also depend on regional interests. For example, there may be more Marvel collectors in one city than another, or there might be a stronger interest in Disney titles on the West Coast than on the East Coast. A shortage of one book may exist in one region, while there may be plenty of the same issue in another part of the country.

So, what can we learn from all these factors? Just this: A comic book is valuable only because someone else wants it. It has no value of its own, except as scrap paper. Always keep in mind that the price of any comic is determined solely by what another individual is willing to pay for it—not what any price guide or dealer's list estimates that it's worth.

The price you pay is what the comic is worth, regardless of what a dealer's price tag or price guide may say. You, the collector, make the comic book valuable.

MAKING MONEY: INVESTING IN COMICS

Collecting and reading comics should be done first for pleasure. But that doesn't mean that you can't make some money from your hobby as well.

If you purchase comic books wisely, take care of them, and hold onto them for a few years, you will get at least your investment back, and you might make a nice chunk of money as well. And if you study the comic book market and plan your collection carefully, you can very easily make a nice profit that will repay you for the time and money you've invested.

Be warned, however: Investing and speculating in comic books is a highly specialized field. You not only have to understand how the comic book marketplace works, you have to be able to think like a collector. Comic book investment is not for the casual speculator or the person who has no interest other than making a fast buck. Most of the successful investors and speculators in the comic field are also comic fans and readers.

If you want to invest a sizable sum in old comic books, wait at least six months to a year. Take that much time to learn about collector interest, comic book artists, and which titles and companies are in demand.

Basic Facts (and a Discouraging Word) About Investing in Comics

Comic books, like other collectibles, such as antiques, rare books, and coins, produce no dividends on your investment. You make money only when you sell the comics, and you must keep your money tied up until you liquidate the books. Not only that, you must take care of your investments.

Comics aren't like gold, silver, stocks, or bonds. They require careful handling and careful storage. A $1,000 comic can become worthless if damaged by heat, humidity, pests, or your own carelessness.

And like other collectibles, comic books are not very "liquid." If you want to get money for your comics, you first have to find a buyer. You

96

can't walk into a bank with a copy of Spider-Man #1 and expect to pay off this month's mortgage. For some comics, it make take months or even years to find a suitable buyer. Obviously, you don't want to tie up needed cash in comic books.

Finally, to invest in comic books, you usually have to buy them at retail prices, yet you must sell at wholesale. For example, suppose you buy a comic for $100 from a dealer. If you take that same book in the very next day, he'll probably be able to buy it back from you for only $50. You're going to have to wait until the book is worth at least $200 retail before you can sell it for $100 wholesale and recoup your initial investment.

If all of this sounds discouraging—good. Too many casual collectors have charged gung ho into investing and speculating in comic books, without realizing that to show a profit, one has to have patience, luck, and a lot of savvy.

But there is some good news. The proper comic books purchased in nice condition can offer a respectable return on your money. And there are fantastic profits that can be made on the right books, bought and sold at the right times. I've known several comic book investors who've made more money during the last decade than many of the country's gold traders. There are very few other markets where you can make a 10,000-percent profit on a six-month investment, yet you can with comic books. And even if you buy conservatively, yet wisely, you should be able to get a 10–20-percent annual return on all the money you invest. That ain't bad.

Buying for Investment

Buying comics for investment is a little different than buying for pleasure or for your own collection. Collectors usually buy comics that they themselves enjoy. Investors buy comics that others enjoy and want—the popular and mainstay titles.

For a safe investment, buy comics that have a past history of being highly collected and valued. Which comics are the most widely sought after? Marvel and DC comics have always made up the majority of collectible titles. For the last 25 years, over 80 percent of the business done in comic books has been in Marvel and DC titles. Traditionally, some of the most widely collected titles from these two publishers have been:

Action	*Green Lantern*
Adventure	*Incredible Hulk*
Amazing Spider-Man	*Iron Man*
Avengers	*Justice League of America*
Batman	*Legion of Superheroes*

Conan	New Teen Titans
Daredevil	Superman
Fantastic Four	Thor
Flash	X-Men

Of course, there are, and will be, many more titles from Marvel and DC that collectors value. The above titles, however, have a history of collector interest. The investor should also be alert for developing activity in other titles from these two publishers. Significantly, only Marvel and DC comics are usually included in biannual price-guide updates, since prices change more rapidly on these comics than on those from other publishers.

There are many other comics, however, that are also worthy of investor consideration. Many of the costumed hero comics from the 1940s find a ready market. Comics published by EC in the early 1950s, as well as other books with artwork by highly valued artists from that period, are always in demand. The Disney comics drawn by Carl Barks will always have an appreciative audience, and comics that feature strips and artwork by the long-established newspaper comic-strip artists are definite collector mainstays.

Except for the Disney comics drawn by Carl Barks, however, the majority of investor comics generally fall into these categories:

1. Golden Age hero comics from 1939 to 1947 (Superman, Captain America, Batman, Submariner, Captain Marvel, etc.); specifically DC and Marvel (Timely) hero titles and others from the World War II years especially.

2. EC and other comics from 1950–1954 with artwork by highly collected artists.

3. Early issues of Marvel and DC titles from 1959 to 1964.

Of course, there are many newer comics from the 1970s and 1980s that have made a lot of money for investors, but these books are better described in the section on speculation in comic books, later in this chapter.

Investment-Quality Books

If you just want to read a particular comic, it really doesn't matter what condition it's in, as long as it is complete. If you're buying for investment, however, condition becomes much more important.

So important is the condition of an investment-quality comic that you should never buy a comic specifically for investment unless it is in at least Fine condition. Books in Good or Very Good condition, even when rare and desirable, just do not appreciate as fast as better-grade comics.

Not only that, it is actually harder to sell a scarce book in Good condition than one in Fine or better shape.

Ideally, comics purchased for investment should be in even Near-Mint or Mint condition. This is absolutely essential for comics published in the last 20 years. For older books, from the 1940s through the early 1960s, Fine condition is acceptable for comics bought for investment and resale.

The Long and Short of Comic Book Investment

You can invest in comics either for a short-term return or as a long-term investment. A short-term investment is for three months to two years. A long-term investment period is from three to fifteen years.

If you're going to buy comics simply to make a quick profit within a year or so, you want to buy books for a short-term investment. This is also often called "speculation." Speculation generally involves buying several copies of one issue for a quick resale as the comic increases in value. There is usually an element of risk in speculation and short-term comic book investments.

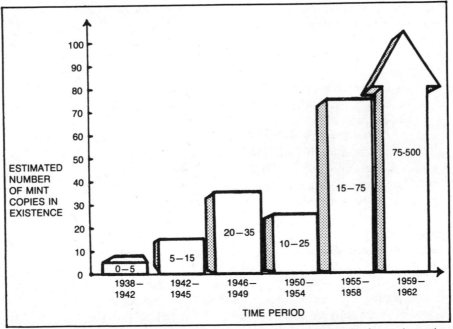

Although no one actually knows the number of existing Mint issues for each comic title, this chart provides an educated estimate. The number of existing mint copies decreased slightly in the early 1950s, due to the reduced print runs. After the early 1960s, mint comics became much more common as collectors started buying and saving them in large quantities. This chart illustrates why top-condition books are a good investment—they are incredibly scarce.

On the other hand, long-term comic book investments are generally safer yet yield a slower return on your money. You can think of a long-term comic book investment as a blue-chip stock—an investment that increases slowly but steadily from year to year.

Because of the peculiarities of the comic market, some books do better as short-term investments while others will show a significant profit only after several years. Before you invest in comics, ask yourself if you want a quick return on your money or if you can keep your money tied up for a longer period. If you buy comics that are good long-term investments but sell them too early, you can lose money. Similarly, it's possible to hold onto certain comics too long and lose profits by not selling them quickly enough.

How can you tell which comics are good money-making short-term investments and which ones will make you more money over a long period? Let's find out.

Comics As a Short-Term Investment (Speculation)

Short-term investment is more accurately described as "speculation." Speculation is a high-risk, high-return proposition. Here's how it works.

To make any significant amount of money from a short-term comic book investment, you will have to hold onto them for at least three months, and more likely for six to eighteen months. Of course, you can turn a profit on a comic in a day if you buy for an immediate resale. I've purchased a comic book at a convention for $25 and resold it within 15 minutes for $50. But that's not an investment; it's just working on a buyer-seller margin.

Except for a very few selected back-issue comics, prices on old books rarely increase enough in a short period for a significant profit. There are exceptions; collector interest in a back-issue title may be revived by a new comic title featuring the same character, or an artist may become so popular that all back issues with his work are in demand.

Most of the money from short-term comic book investments, however, comes from new issues, books that are just published. If you want to speculate or second-guess the comic market, the place to do it is with the new comics as they appear on the newsstand.

Speculating in new comics is usually done like this: You pick out a specific comic title and issue number that you think will probably be a big seller. This may be a first issue of a new title, or it may be an issue that features artwork by a popular artist. It could also be a comic that introduces a new character or features an important change in the comic's story line. Whatever your reason, after you select a comic that you think will go up in value, the next step is to place an order with a distributor or comic subscription service for multiple copies.

Buying just one or two or three issues of a new comic for speculation is usually not worthwhile. Even if the comic doubles or triples in price, you will make only a few dollars. So you will want to buy at least 10 copies of a new comic for speculation, and maybe as many as 200 to 300 copies (300 copies are in a case of new comics). Some large-scale speculators may buy even ten cases or more of one particularly strong comic title, which comes out to 3,000 issues of the same comic.

One reason that such large quantities are bought is that it makes it possible to advertise and resell the same title in large quantities to other collectors and speculators. After all, it is not worthwhile to advertise only five or ten copies of one comic for sale, since the cost of the advertising would eliminate any profits. On the other hand, if you're sitting on ten or more cases of a desirable comic, you can even resell single cases to other speculators and investors for a nice, quick profit.

Another reason to buy many copies of the same comic is that you will get about a 50-percent discount from a wholesaler or distributor if you buy in such quantities. This means that you are paying only half the cover price for the new comic. This offers you some protection, because even if the comic sells for only its face value after a few months, you can still double your money.

Buying large quantities of new comics is much like buying a roll of uncirculated coins or an entire sheet of new stamps. The only difference is that with new comics, you often must place an order with a distributor or wholesaler about two or three months *before* the comic appears. This means that you will have to keep up with forthcoming comics by reading collector publications, fanzines, and the publicity releases of the various comic publishers.

Of course, you can still speculate in new comics just by buying multiple copies of a new comic from your favorite comic book store or newsstand.

Comic Title and Number	Wholesale Price for 100 Issues (dollars)	Retail Price of 100 Issues (dollars)	Number of Months Comics Were Held
Daredevil #158	17.50	1,250.00	42
New Teen Titans #1	25.00	750.00	24
Daredevil #168	25.00	600.00	20
X-Men #125	20.00	200.00	36
X-Men #137	25.00	167.00	24
Marvel Fanfare #1	62.50	200.00	6
Fantastic Four #232	25.00	50.00	14
Spider-Man #252	30.00	400.00	3

If you do this, however, you must pay full cover price for the comic, which will decrease your profits.

So how much money can you make by speculating in new comics? A lot. If you choose right. Consider some of these examples of money made from recent comics by speculators.

Here's what the above table means: If you just invested $17.50 in 100 issues of *Daredevil #158* when it first appeared, and then waited for 42 months (3½ years later), you could potentially sell the 100 copies for more than $1,200 profit! That figures out to a 7,142-percent on your investment—much better than gold, silver, diamonds, or any other collectible item for that period. If you bought (and sold) *Spider-Man #252* at the right time, you would have realized better than a 1,000 percent return in less than three months!

However, keep this in mind: The same month that *Daredevil #158* or *Spider-Man #252* appeared, there were also about 100 other comic titles on the newsstand. Most of these other comics did absolutely nothing in the collector market. If you bought 100 copies of all these other titles, you probably would have made almost nothing on your investment, and you could even have lost money on some of the books.

Why was *Daredevil #158* a hit and all the other comics that month a miss? Primarily because that issue of *Daredevil* marked the first appearance of artwork by Frank Miller on that title. Miller later became a highly sought-after artist in the fan marketplace, and all comics with his art started selling very well. A few lucky speculators anticipated that Miller would become popular with the collectors and bought heavily of this particular issue. Most people did not.

And that brings up another important point in speculating in new comics: Don't follow the herd. If everybody is buying up large quantities of a new comic, there will be a sufficient supply to meet the anticipated demand, and the price will not go up rapidly. Your best chance of making money on new comics is to outguess the other speculators and investors and store away a potential bestseller that others have overlooked.

What are the signs of a potentially "hot" comic title? The first is a new artist or writer who displays great talent. If this artist's or writer's output continues to improve and find favor with collectors, they will want to seek out the first appearances by these creative people. Of course, a new artist may also fizzle or quit the comics field, in which case his books will not be in as much demand. When you speculate on a new artist, you're gambling that he's going to be an even bigger success later. If he does, you win. If not, you take a loss.

Another factor that can turn a new comic into a highly desirable back issue is the introduction of a new character or a major change in the comic's story line. Quite often a new character will be introduced into a comic as an experiment. If the readers like the character, then he or she may be given his or her own comic book. In these cases, the early appearances of this character become highly desirable.

Also, an important change in a comic's story line, such as the death of a major supporting character, can spell high collector demand for the book. Sometimes, however, it's easy to overestimate the importance of a story-line change when gauging potential collector interest. For example, speculators went crazy over *Spider-Man #252* that simply featured a temporary costume change. The market later adjusted, and the prices fell for this particular issue.

One other danger for the speculator in new comics is the fascination with #1 issues. Almost every first issue of a new title is now bought in such large quantities by speculators, fans, and casual collectors that the supply will almost always outlast the demand. Everybody knows that #1 issues are potentially valuable, and because they are bought in such large quantities for that very reason, they ironically become more common than the second or third issue of a title. The only time you should invest heavily in #1 issues of new comics is when you think that the title has a truly strong potential for developing into a real fan favorite, such as was the case with *The New Teen Titans #1*.

Speculating in new comics is very appealing for a number of reasons. Perhaps the best reason is that, unlike older and rare back issues, new comics are available to everyone. It would be very difficult, for example, to stockpile a quantity of *X-Men Comics #1*. Not only would the price be high for such old issues, but locating the books in the first place would be very time consuming. New comics are as easy to find as this month's order form from a comic distributor.

Not only that, but new comics may be purchased at wholesale prices and at a low enough price so that there is plenty of room for the price to grow and increase rapidly. For example, new comics may be purchased in quantity for about 40–50 cents each. It is not unreasonable for a new comic to suddenly be selling for $2 or $3 a few months later, if collector interest develops. You have more of a profit margin to work with on new comics, and there is plenty of room for the title to grow in price.

There are risks. It is harder to sell 300 copies of the same issue than it is to sell a single copy of one rare comic. And don't forget: There are hundreds of other collectors, investors, and speculators who are also trying to second-guess the new-comic market and outguess each other at the same time. Remember, after all, that speculation is defined as "a business deal where a good profit can be made at considerable risk."

Long-Term Investments in Comics

Unlike speculation in new comics, where you buy in quantity and sell a few months later, long-term comic book investments require you to carefully select a single issue of an older comic and hold onto it for a number of years as it steadily increases in value.

This is a safer and more conservative approach to comic investing. It does take longer and the profits may be lower, but the risks are much less.

A long-term investment works like this: You select a high-quality, high-price book, such as a near-mint copy of *Fantastic Four #1*. You store it carefully away for anywhere from three to six years, and then you resell it.

Most investment-quality comics appreciate at the rate of 20–40 percent per year. This means that after three or four years, your book will have doubled in value. Remember, however, that if you sell the book at wholesale prices to a dealer, you will probably receive only 50 percent of its retail value. This means that after three or four years, you're only breaking even.

If you hold onto the comic for another three years or six years total, then you can realize a 50–60 percent profit, even if you sell the comic at wholesale. This works out to a 10-percent or better annual return on your investment.

The trick is to sell investment-quality comics at retail prices to other

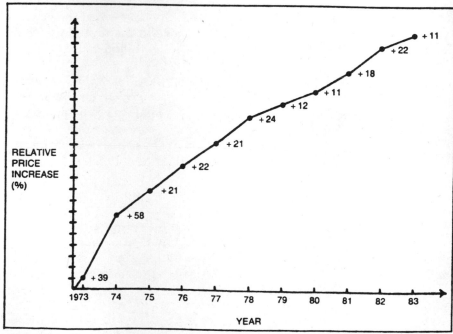

This chart illustrates the yearly average price increases for a selected range of comic titles.

104

collectors and bypass the wholesale market. This way you can double your profits and turn a respectable investment into an excellent one. Selling high-quality comics on a one-to-one basis to other collectors is not that difficult in the comic market, and we'll tell you how in chapter 10.

Deciding which books to buy for long-term investment requires that you study the past performances of high-value comics over the last several years. And it also means that you must be something of a prophet— you have to be able to predict which books you think will be worth more four, five, or six years later, when it comes time to sell your investment. Studying the past and predicting the future are all part of learning about the market trends in comic books.

Trends in Comic Book Collecting

Why does a comic book that no one wanted one year suddenly become a bestseller the next year? And why does a comic that had been a hot item and going up, up, up in price become a dog, a turkey, and a drag on the market? If you know the answers to these questions, you can make a lot of money buying and selling comics.

Like all speculative investments, comic books follow a definite trend, or pattern of price increases and decreases, from year to year. One year, a comic title or artist or even a comic company may capture the interest of fans and collectors and the prices for these books may suddenly sky rocket. For one or two or three years, collector interest in this particular area may become intense, with higher and higher offers being made for these books. And then one day, the investor or collector who purchased these books may find that no one is interested anymore in yesterday's bestseller.

Spotting and forecasting collecting trends is the hardest yet most profitable activity for a comic book investor or speculator. Fortunately, there are some general guidelines and collecting history that will help you anticipate which trend is coming up and which one is on the way out.

Looking to the Past

Those who do not learn from history are doomed to repeat the mistakes of the past. Such is the sage advice given to students who want a good reason for studying history in school. It's also a good reason to study the history of comic collecting trends. While past trends in comic collecting cannot predict future trends, you can learn a lot about how the comic market behaves if you study market activity and collector interest over the last several years.

First we'll look at some of the *general* market trends from the last several years on an annual basis:

1975. During this year, collectors expressed a strong interest in early Marvel and Timely comics (Timely was the name for Marvel comics published during the 1940s). The rarer Silver Age DC comics (comics from 1959 to 1964) were also sought after. EC comics, which had enjoyed a strong market the previous five years, were now cooling off and holding steady. Most of the Golden Age comics (those published from 1938 to 1949) were selling slowly. Comics that had artwork by Carl Barks (Donald Duck), Walt Kelly (Pogo), Wally Wood (EC comics), and Basil Wolverton (early 1950s science-fiction titles) were selling very well this year.

1976. A good year for comic sales. Almost all the Timely comics increased 40–60 percent in value, and Spider-Man comics were up by 75 percent. Almost every "key" comic book (that is, a #1 issue, origin issue, or special issue) went up 25–35 percent over 1975 prices. Books in demand included all ECs, Disney comics, Silver Age DCs and Marvels, and comics with artwork by Frank Frazetta, Wally Wood, Walt Kelly, and Basil Wolverton. Comics from the 1940s and 1950s that featured pinup art and heroines were termed "Good Girl Art" comics, and these sold extremely well in 1976. During this year, the price for a comic in Mint condition was *three* times the price for its Good-condition counterpart; until 1976, a Mint comic usually had sold for about twice the price of a Good comic.

1977. Again the strong-selling comics were those that featured Good Girl Art, as well as artwork by Walt Kelly and Basil Wolverton. Silver Age DC and Marvel comics were still in high demand. Disney comics, EC comics, and comics published by Avon, particularly the science-fiction titles, increased in value. The top-selling titles this year increased around 35 percent on the average, with Uncle Scrooge one of the fastest-increasing comic values, at a 58 percent increase over the previous year.

1978. After two years of increasing interest, comics featuring Good Girl Art really took off, with prices doubling and tripling for selected issues. Fiction House Comics, a publisher from the 1940s and early 1950s known for its emphasis on pinup art and jungle heroines, became a strong seller. All science-fiction titles, particularly those published by EC and Avon, sold very well. A new interest was developing in comics from the late 1940s to 1954, the precode years, and collectors were searching for comics that had been mentioned in a book called *Seduction of the Innocent* because of their violent and sexually suggestive scenes. In contrast to the previous years, interest was down in the Silver Age comics, from 1959 to

1964. On the other hand, Golden Age comics, which had been in a slump, were picking up steam. The Donald Duck books by Carl Barks increased an incredible 105 percent, and Archie comics, long ignored by collectors, posed a 47-percent gain.

1979. This was the year for the early 1950s precode comics. Record prices were paid for comics that had been mentioned in *Seduction of the Innocent* and for comics from 1949 to 1954 that had scenes of violence and drug use. Science-fiction and horror comics were in high demand. Comics with Good Girl artwork were slowing down; they increased only about 20 percent in value, as compared to a 50-percent jump in prices the previous year. There was renewed interest in top-quality Golden Age books on the part of investors who were looking for a hedge against the high inflation of that year. And, perhaps most significant of all, a relatively recent comic, the new *X-Men* title from Marvel, which had first been revived in 1975, suddenly grabbed collector interest.

1980. This was the year of the X-Men. Prices for *X-Men #94* and the giant-size *X-Men #1,* both published only five years previously, went crazy. Dealers were hiking their asking price for the X-Men books on a monthly basis, and still the fans were buying. On the other hand, many of the other recent Marvels and all the Silver Age comics of the last 15 years were selling very slowly. Prices also slowed on the comics from the 1950s, especially the Good Girl Art books, *Seduction of the Innocent* comics, and science-fiction titles. Much interest was also focused on DC comics from the 1940s, and Captain Marvel, which had sold poorly the past several years, picked up slightly.

1981. Comics published from 1964 to 1976 were slowing down in sales as collectors began to concentrate on either the more recent titles such as the *New Teen Titans, X-Men,* and Frank Miller's *Daredevil,* or the books from the 1950s, particularly DCs and horror comics. Sales continued to drop for Avon comics, Good Girl Art comics, and other special-artist issues from the early 1950s. A renewed interest in Golden Age comics was also evident.

1982. Comics published from 1965 to 1980 continued to drop in price, with dealers reporting an overstock in all areas. On the other hand, the newer titles published after 1980 developed strong collector interest. The only strong demand for comics published from the 1950s was for science-fiction and horror comics and comics with artwork by Steve Ditko and Wally Wood. DC comics from 1938 to 1964 sold very well, but most of the older comics, from 1940 to 1960, remained steady in price or increased only slightly. Collectors seemed to concentrate more and more on the new releases and the specialty comics sold only in comic book stores.

1983. Another year for strong interest in the new-comic market. Collectors seemed to be spending more and more of their collecting dollar on the many new comic releases and ignoring the back-issue books of ten to twenty years ago as a consequence. Significantly, prices on many older comics from all eras remained stable or even decreased slightly when adjusted for inflation. Golden Age books in top condition, however, sold very well, and investment-quality books in mint grades became harder and harder to find. All DC comics from 1940 to 1964 sold very well. Timely (Marvel) comics from the 1940s and most science-fiction comics from the 1950s enjoyed brisk sales. A lot of the back-issue activity, however, was in books published in the last five to ten years, as the new collectors sought to complete the collections they started with the current comic titles.

What can we learn from these yearly trends? First, the comic book market is always in a stage of compensation and adjustment. For one or two years, prices may increase rapidly in one collecting area while remaining steady or slow in other areas. Then the slow-moving comics may suddenly become more in demand, and their prices will move up to adjust to the new popularity. Meanwhile, the comics that had been shooting up in price will start to slow down as the price of the comics begins to reflect the true interest in the title.

Here's a real example of how the prices fluctuate and adjust themselves in the comic marketplace. In the mid-1970s, there was a tremendous interest in Marvel comics from the early 1960s. Consequently prices started to rise rapidly, and some Marvel issues increased in value by 50–75 percent within a single year. These price increases continued for early Marvels for another two years. At the same time, DC comics from the same period (1961–1964) remained at fixed or lower prices. After three years of rapid price increase for Marvels and little or no increase for DC comics, collectors suddenly realized that DC comics were underpriced in comparison to the expensive Marvel books.

As a result, collectors saw the DC comics as a better bargain when compared to the Marvel comics. Interest moved over to the DC comics, and then prices for them started to increase while the Marvel comics remained at a slowly increasing or fixed price level.

Collectors and investors do follow trends in comics. As a comic begins to increase in price, more and more people start to buy it, which further increases the price. At a certain point, collectors believe that the comic has become overpriced in comparison to similar comics, and interest falls off. The trick is to anticipate a trend before it starts to take off and to get in while the prices are still low.

Price Increases and Fluctuations

Let's look at the comic marketplace over the last ten years to get a general idea of how comics have performed as an investment. First we'll look at the top ten most valuable comic titles from 1972 and then compare them to the top ten for 1983.

Ten Most Valuable Comics (1972 Value)

Title	Comment
1. *Detective*	features Batman
2. *Adventure*	DC comic, published 1930s–1980s
3. *More Fun*	DC comic from the 1940s
4. *Action*	features Superman
5. *King*	newspaper-strip reprints; Flash Gordon
6. *Famous Funnies*	Buck Rogers; other strip reprints
7. *Marvel Mystery*	Captain America; other Marvel heroes
8. *Walt Disney*	Donald Duck by Carl Barks
9. *All Star*	features Golden Age DC heroes
10. *Popular*	newspaper reprints; Dick Tracy

Eleven years later, the list looked something like this:

Ten Most Valuable comics (1983 Value)

Title

1. *Action*

2. *Marvel Mystery*

3. *Detective*

4. *More Fun*

5. *Superman*

6. *Adventure*

7. *Whiz* (Captain Marvel)

8. *Captain America*

9. *Donald Duck*

10. *Walt Disney*

ular, comic books featuring reprinted newspaper strips decreased dramatically in popularity. Notice also that *Marvel Mystery* and *Captain America,* two major Timely/Marvel titles, made the list in 1983, which demonstrates the strong collector interest in Golden Age Marvel comics.

Now, to get a good overall picture of the comic market for an 11-year period, we'll combine both the 1972 and 1983 most valuable comic titles into one list. We'll look at how the prices for these titles increased from year to year and see the overall average price increase per year for each title.

Percentage of Price Increases of Selected Golden Age Titles

Title	Percentage Increase from Previous Year											
	1973	1974	1975	1976	1977	1978	1979	1980	1981	1982	1983	Avg
Detective	37	57	26	30	15	19	11	18	26	30	19	26
Adventure	30	32	10	18	26	13	18	22	27	26	20	22
More Fun	24	33	31	21	40	22	16	10	25	24	13	23
Action	56	128	11	20	36	23	8	15	23	28	11	33
King	22	−10	2	0	8	4	15	4	5	34	15	9
Famous Funnies	21	3	9	4	23	5	20	3	3	−5	5	9
Marvel Mystery	47	107	35	58	27	24	1	12	15	25	17	33
Walt Disney	53	58	27	19	19	22	7	14	15	10	1	22
All Star	20	40	24	21	9	18	13	14	35	30	16	21
Popular	14	−7	3	0	10	7	(Almost No Change)					3
Superman	44	77	18	25	24	31	29	29	29	29	15	32
Donald Duck	94	66	54	24	31	105	15	−2	14	14	−7	38
Whiz	64	142	27	21	10	24	0	0	17	22	9	30
Captain America	26	85	23	44	20	20	11	17	12	35	14	27
Yearly Average	39	58	21	22	21	24	12	11	18	22	11	24

Studying the chart, we first notice that, on the average, comic book prices increased almost 25 percent per year for the more popular titles. Actually, the market has been growing a little more slowly than that in the last four or five years.

Notice that the DC (*Superman, Action*) and the Marvel (*Marvel Mystery, Captain America*) comics from the 1940s have been consistently high performers. One of the most rapidly increasing comics in value was the *Donald Duck* title drawn by Carl Barks (up a whopping 105 percent in one year), but in the last several years this title's prices have stabilized at a much slower rate of increase.

There are other comic titles that have performed better than those listed above, and there are many other older comics that have not done as well. The titles selected above merely reflect general market trends. The percentage of increase (or decrease) is based on the total estimated retail value of a complete collection for each title listed.

Investment-quality books do not have to come from the Golden Age of comics (1940s). Certain comics from the late 1950s and early 1960s (called the Silver Age of comics) have performed just as well as (and in some cases better than) the older comics. Let's look at the bestselling Silver Age comic titles from the early 1960s in the two lists that follow.

Ten Most Valuable Silver Age Titles (1971 Value)

1. *Showcase*

2. *Fantastic Four*

3. *Brave and Bold*

4. *Jimmy Olsen*

5. *Tales to Astonish* (Hulk)

6. *Spider-Man*

7. *Flash*

8. *Challengers of the Unknown*

9. *My Greatest Adventure* (Doom Patrol)

10. *Journey into Mystery* (Thor)

Ten Most Valuable Silver Age Titles (1983 Value)

1. *Showcase*

2. *Fantastic Four*

3. *Spider-Man*

4. *Brave and Bold*

5. *Flash*

6. *Richie Rich*

7. *Tales to Astonish* (Hulk)

8. *Jimmy Olsen*

9. *Justice League of America*

10. *Green Lantern*

The first thing you'll probably notice is that, on both lists, only one comic (Richie Rich) is not either a Marvel or a DC title. DC has six titles on each list, while Marvel has four titles for 1971 and three for 1983.

Prices of these Silver Age comics generally are significantly lower than for the Golden Age comics of the 1940s. However, there are a few comics from the early 1960s that cost $300–1,000. Let's look at how prices have increased for a selected lot of Silver Age comics over a four-year period:

Percentage of Price Increases of Selected Silver Age Titles

Title	Percentage Increase from Previous Year					
	1979	1980	1981	1982	1983	Average
Showcase	40	31	30	11	2	23
Fantastic Four	38	21	18	12	2	18
Spider-Man	28	50	15	12	8	23
Brave and Bold	39	37	30	19	3	26
Flash	44	22	17	14	−6	18
Jimmy Olsen	8	33	22	32	7	20
Tales to Astonish	38	35	22	11	1	21
Yearly Average	34	33	22	16	2	22

The significantly depressed price increases for 1983 reflect the increased collector interest in new comic releases over the older comics of 20 years ago.

It is interesting to note that both the top-selling Golden Age comics and the bestselling Silver Age comics have maintained about the same overall annual increase in value: 20–25 percent on the average.

Which Comics to Invest In: Building Your Portfolio

As you invest in rare comics, it's important to have an overall plan. At first, it's best to specialize in one area, such as Golden Age DC comics or Silver Age Marvel books. This way you can learn how the market is going and which comics have the best potential for growth. Another good reason to specialize is that when it comes time to sell, you may have an easier time advertising and selling comics that appeal to a special group of collectors and dealers. For example, it may be easier to dispose of a single nice Batman collection that it would be to sell a hodgepodge of random titles.

On the other hand, it is equally important to diversify your investments. If you tied up all your money in early issues of *Spider-Man,* you might find that someday nobody is at all interested in that particular title and you'd have a hard time selling.

You probably should protect yourself and invest some of your money in the "classic," or blue-chip, books of the comic field: early, nice-condition comics that feature Marvel or DC heroes from the 1940s. You should also include a good smattering of Marvel or DC Silver Age comics from the early 1960s, particularly #1 issues in Near-Mint or better condition.

You should also sink some cash into high-risk comics that might provide a high return. For example, few collectors several years ago thought that early issues of *Richie Rich* comics would ever be worth anything. Yet that title came out of nowhere and rapidly went up, up, and up in price. Similarly, I invested in many issues of *Donald Duck* back in the late 1960s when almost no one was interested in the title. I made a 3,000-percent return on my money when I sold them six years later. So risk taking is certainly advisable on some comic books. Just don't tie up all your money on longshot books.

Finally, if you keep up with the current marketplace, you may want to try a little speculation with one or two selected titles. If you believe that a forthcoming issue has good investment potential, buy a case of 300 copies from a wholesaler and store it away for a few months or several years. If you pick right, you could make a few hundred or several thousand dollars. If you don't . . . well, you'll have 299 duplicates to trade for the next 20 years!

A Final Word on Comic Book Investments

Investing in your hobby can be an exciting and fun way to put your extra money to work for you. Having issues of old and rare comics is so much more satisfying than owning a stock certificate or government bond; however, don't fool yourself.

Many collectors use the investment aspect of comics simply as an excuse to overindulge in their hobby and to spend more money than they can afford. You should not put all your investment capital in comics any more than you should tie up all of your money in commodities, oil wells, gold, or utility bonds. Most investment specialists advise that only 20–25 percent of your extra capital be put in collectibles of any sort. The rest should be diversified among more conventional options.

And be warned that the comic book market is still a relatively young child. It does not yet have the history or "respectability" of the older collectibles, such as coins, stamps, or antiques. Just as significant, much of the money spent on comics is from "low-end" investors—people with limited funds to spend. In contrast, the stamp and coin markets cater to consortiums, syndicates, banks, and other investment institutions with large amounts of disposable capital.

Finally, you had better know a lot about comics before you start sinking money into them. A simple thing such as a newly reprinted issue of an old comic book can catch the unwary investor off guard and depress the market for the original edition of that particular book.

For the collector, reader, and fan who knows the comic book field, however, investing in comics is a fine and fun way of making enough money to support your hobby, and perhaps even your family. And admit it: You're just looking for a good reason to buy some more comics anyway, aren't you?

WHAT ARE YOUR COMICS REALLY WORTH?

Comic collecting is a simple enough hobby. You buy books you like to read, you save them, you buy some more, and eventually you sell them. But for all the simplicity, there is one difficult area in comic collecting that confuses both the beginning and the experienced collector.

Nobody really knows what his comic collection is worth.

Oh sure, you can sit down with a price guide or dealer's catalog and figure up what your collection would be worth if you could sell every comic for this or that price. But the truth is, you won't be able to sell all your comics for fair market value. In fact, there is so much confusion about what a comic is worth that you may be unable to get even a vague idea of what your comics are really worth.

To add to the confusion, collectors see ever-increasing prices being asked for back-issue comics. They pull out the latest issue of a comic book price guide and see the high prices that their comics are supposedly worth. They see big price tags stuck on comics for sale.

It is a tempting illusion to sit back and believe that all your comics stashed safely away in your closet are making you rich. But it could be only an illusion. Let's try to clear the air about comic book values and prices so you'll have a better understanding of what your collection is really worth.

Appreciation Rate of Comic Books

First off, does comic collecting pay? If you believe newspaper and magazine articles, you will answer *yes!* And if you follow trends in the comic book price guides and dealer's catalogs, you will also believe that wealth awaits those who will sell their ever-more-valuable collections. It's hard not to believe that comic collecting is a high-profit hobby.

For example, on paper, comic books look like a dynamite investment. If you study the price increases of the fifty most valuable comic titles over a period of ten years, you'll find out that comic books are a better investment than gold, stamps, coins, rare books, and probably even illicit drugs.

Look at the following table. You'll see that a wise assortment of comic books purchased in 1971 could have yielded an almost 600-percent return!

Ten-Year Appreciation Rate of Selected Collectibles

Investment	Appreciation Rate, 1970–1980 (percent)
Coins	16.0
Rare Books	16.1
Ceramics	18.8
Stamps	21.8
Gold	31.6
Comic Books*	582.4

* Fifty most valuable comic titles, 1970–1980

Of course, figures lie. If such an appreciation rate were real, then there would be no old comics or back issues left; they would have all been bought up by wealthy investors and bankers who recognize a sure money-making proposition.

The prices in official guides routinely hide the reality of comic book values from the casual fan and collector. The difference between the value of a comic in a price guide and its actual buying and selling prices can be unsettling to the person who takes his comics to market for the first time.

So what is the "real" comic market? And what are your comics "really" worth?

"Basically, a comic book is worth exactly what another person will pay you for it," is the advice that a manager and partner in several comic book specialty shops told me.

A dealer buys for resale. If the comic won't sell, why buy it? And believe me, there are tons and tons of comics that don't sell. Here's a classic example: Howard the Duck *comics. A few years ago, they sold moderately well. Now it's a cause for celebration if I can sell the first issue for anywhere near guide. So how can you explain to the kid collector who wants you to buy his* Howard the Duck *collection that it's now basically worthless and you don't want it at any price?*

Many collectors are shocked when they bring their collections to comic book stores and dealers and they are offered less than the face value of the comics. Many times, their collection consists just of the books they've liked and bought off the racks for the past five years or so. Still, getting back less money than you paid for a comic always seems a little hard to take, until you understand the economics of comic buying and selling.

"We cannot pay more than 50 percent of guide price for any comic," another comic dealer explained to me.

And that's just for hot comics we know we can immediately resell. Any retail store has to operate on that 50-percent margin—the difference between what you buy a book for and what you can sell it for. Most retail businesses work on that margin, and if you do not regularly sell books for at least twice what you paid for them, you'll be out of business.

Most comic dealers price their books at full guide value. Does that mean they are paying 50 percent for all old comic books—including the ones tucked away in your closet?

"No way can I give half of guide for most Golden Age comic books [those published in the 1940s]," another major comic-store owner stated.

I can't even sell them at half of guide. You'll notice there are few Golden Age comics in my store. That's because I can only afford to offer a fraction of the guide price for them. The owners of such books usually refuse to sell them for that, unless they need money badly. I'll always pay half what I can sell a book for. I'm not trying to be greedy and do collectors out of their books, but it's suicide to believe you can buy and sell comic books at full guide prices—especially for the older stuff that has a specialized market anyway.

Well, you still don't know what your comics are really worth. But you should know by now that they are not worth full guide prices, at least not to a dealer.

The Six Different Values of a Comic Book

The problem is this: There is no one value for a back-issue comic book. In fact, just about every comic book in your collection has at least *six* different values! So hang on, you're about to get a graduate course in comic book economics.

Salvage Price

Salvage has an unpleasant sound to it. It sounds like automobile junkyards or sunken ships. Yet your comic books have a basic salvage value.

Salvage actually means "to save from destruction." The salvage value of your collection is what you can get for it as junked goods instead of just destroying them or throwing them away.

Currently, the salvage value of used comics is anywhere from 10 to 20 cents apiece—that's based on the resale value of a used comic at half its new price. In other words, if you walk into most used bookstores, flea markets, or resale shops, you would expect to get about 10 cents each for your old comics. So, if you want to junk your collection, you can always get the salvage price.

For such a small return, you would probably want to keep the collection just to read again or to give to someone else who would appreciate it. This points out the second value level of your comics: their *intrinsic worth*.

Intrinsic Worth

Every collectible has an intrinsic worth. For example, a rare penny may be worth a hundred dollars to a coin collector, but its intrinsic, or actual worth, is 1 cent.

The intrinsic worth of a comic book is simply what the book is worth to read. In other words, new comic books sell for 75 cents to $1 because people consider them worth that much just to read.

A comic book always has an intrinsic value. Your collection, then, always has a built-in value. This value is roughly the retail price of a new comic times the number of comics you have. Still, it may be hard to get even the intrinsic value of your collection in hard cash.

"Surprisingly enough," says a major mail-order dealer,

> *There is actually a mathematically finite limit of how many* Dazzler *#10's I can sell. If I have a hundred copies in the back room, it's hard to get excited about buying another copy from a collector at any price. And besides that, since most dealers get their new comics direct, we can build a stock of all back-issue comics at below the cover price. That's the thing that blows some collectors' minds, when you tell them that you can't even pay cover price for a back-issue comic book. And not every comic book has a collector's value. Quite often, a book is worth more just to read and reread than it is to try to sell.*

So far, this may be a little depressing. Either you can sell your collection for salvage at 10 cents a comic, or you can reread them until they fall apart or—you can go to the third level of values for your comics: the *support prices* for back issues.

Support Price

Every collectible item, be it a comic book or a matchbook cover or a china doll, has a support price. This simply means that there is always some price at which the dealers will support the market. For example, I may have a thousand-dollar comic book (by the guide value), but I probably can't sell the book for that much. There is some price, however, at which that thousand-dollar comic will always sell to a dealer. It may be $500 or $100 or $10, but there is a support price for all legitimate collectibles.

So, what's the support price for old comic books? What price will a comic book always sell at?

Currently, the support price for all back-issue comics is around 20–25 percent of their guide value. This figure is based on the national advertising "buy" prices of several major comic brokers. These brokers state in their ads and lists that they will buy almost any comic listed in the price guide at 25 percent of its value. In other words, they are guaranteeing that your comics are worth at least one-fourth the current guide value, and they will immediately purchase them for that amount.

Of course, after you list and grade all your comics and take the added expense of mailing the comics to these dealers and brokers, you are probably realizing only about 20 percent of the guide prices for your books.

The true market support for old comics, then, is around 20–25 percent of their guide value. Even at this level, there is no assurance that all your comics will be purchased. There may be cases of severe overstocking, so that even at low prices the books are not attractive. I myself have advertised comic books in national publications at 15–25 percent of their guide value and have not been able to sell them.

Still, there are usually reputable comic book brokers who will buy the majority of your collection at around one-fifth of guide value. I spoke to one such broker, who told me:

> If I can't pay 20 percent for any back-issue comic and not make a profit, eventually, then either one of two things is going on: one, the price guide is a total lie, which it isn't; or two, the market has dropped out and the guide hasn't had a chance to reflect those changes. I think that for comic collecting to be a legitimate hobby and for the guide to be well respected, you have to have some sort of base support price for back-issue comic books.

Another comic dealer, who has owned and operated four comic book stores over the past 20 years, agrees:

A collector should always be able to take his collection to a dealer and receive a fair price for his books. I have seen dealers advertise some books at, say, twenty dollars apiece. But if you offer them the same books at two or three dollars, they'll refuse to buy them. Now what kind of market is that? I mean, if they're asking twenty bucks for a book, they should fall all over themselves to buy copies at two or three dollars. Yet they don't. This should tell you that you are being played for a sucker. It means that their books aren't worth that price if they won't offer some support in the form of 'buy' prices. Coin dealers, antique dealers, all legitimate collectible dealers know that there is an underlying support price for a market. It shouldn't be any different for comic dealers.

And that brings us to the next value level of your comics: the *buy price*.

Buy Price

Basically, a buy price is what an honest dealer can offer you for a comic. We've already seen that in most cases this is up to 50 percent of what he can sell a comic for. The buy price for most comics by a dealer is 25–50 percent of guide value—if the dealer has the cash and can use the book. The buy price is always a little higher than the support price offered by comic brokers and wholesalers.

On the average, the buy price for a collectible comic is around 35 percent of its guide value. Of course, there are some books that will never bring more than their 20–25-percent support value, no matter what dealer you try. There are a few books that dealers will pay 75–100 percent of guide for, but this buy price simply reflects a retail price that is already above guide value.

Sell Price

This brings up the fifth value level of a comic book: its *sell price*. This is the price that you could get for your comics if you were a dealer or if you sold directly to other collectors. Normally, this is the highest price you can expect for your comics. Generally, most back-issue comics sell for 50–100 percent of the guide value. On average, a back-issue comic usually sells for about 75 percent of guide. This figure is in line with the approximate 35-percent buy figure used by dealers, since it reflects the markup dealers must use to make their margin.

Price-Guide Value

The final value of a comic book is one most people are familiar with: the price-guide value. This value is good for three things: (1) as a basis to use in figuring these other values; (2) as a guide for trading comics of equal value; and (3) as a reference for insurance purposes. It is *not* a good value to use in figuring the true worth of your collection or what you will get for it when it is sold.

Let's look at the six values a comic book can have and what they may mean to you:

Value Level	Cash Value	Comments
Salvage	5–15 cents per comic	Only damaged and junk comics should be sold at this price.
Intrinsic	60–75 cents per comic	The replacement cost of a new comic; may not be actual cash value.
Support	20 percent of guide value	Guaranteed amount a reputable broker will offer you.
Buy	35 percent of guide value	Can vary from 10 to 100 percent, depending on book's demand in market.
Sell	75 percent of guide value	Price paid for a back-issue comic by most collectors.
Guide	100 percent of guide value	Often the "asking" retail price for moderate-demand books.

What can you learn from these values and the chart above? The first thing you can see is that if any comic you have is worth less than a dollar in the price guide, it basically has no collector value. In other words, a used book store may offer you as much for such a comic (salvage value) as you could get from a broker or dealer.

In fact, a comic book generally must be worth at least $2–3 to make it worthwhile to sell it to anyone but a collector. What this means is that unless you are badly pressed for cash, you would be better off keeping all comics worth under $2–3 just for their intrinsic value (unless, of course, you either run completely out of room or suddenly develop a strong aversion to comic books in general).

So, what are your comic books really worth? Well, everybody knows that they are priceless anyway. What else can offer you hours of adventure and fun for so low a price? What other hobby can give you such a deep satisfaction of discovery?

But if you're talking American cash, your comic books are worth only what the next collector or dealer will pay you. And that may be 10 cents, or 10 percent of guide, or 110 percent.

If all this sounds confusing, it is. Comic book prices, like prices for all collectibles, do not follow any hard-and-fast rules. Most people who deal in comics for a living rely a lot on instinct, savvy, and know-how that comes only from being in the marketplace for a number of years.

But have faith. The next chapter will offer some pointers from these professionals for when you finally decide to (gasp!) sell your collection.

CASH FROM COMICS: SELLING YOUR COLLECTION

You thought you'd never do it. But there will come a time when you will sell part or all of your comic collection. When you do, you'll want to get the best price possible, and that's what this chapter is all about: how to sell your comics for the most profit.

Collectors often hate to sell their comics—even if they have lost interest in the books, they still have fond memories associated with the comics in their collection. As a result, a collector who finally decides to part with his collection may make two mistakes: (1) he'll ask far too much for the comics because deep down he's hoping that he won't sell them; or (2) he'll decide to get rid of them all at once to make it less painful, and so he'll dump his collection at a fraction of its true worth.

Selling takes planning, and even if you're convinced now that you will never sell any of your comics, you should still know about the mechanics of selling your collection.

All or Nothing?

You can sell your comics and still have a collection. In fact, the most successful comic collectors often sell parts of their collections every year. Selling a part of your collection allows you to weed out the titles you are no longer interested in and to get money for other comics that you want more.

You can even turn over your entire collection by selling off comics selectively and replacing them with other books. At the end of a few months (or years), you'll have an entirely different collection that was financed entirely by converting your old collection.

So it makes sense to sell *selectively* all through your collecting career. Not only will such selling help build your collection, it will also give you valuable experience should you ever decide to sell out completely.

When Is the Best time to Sell?

The best time to sell your comic books is: (1) when you don't need the money; and (2) while you're still interested.

Most collectors, unfortunately, dispose of their collection when they have to raise some quick cash or when they have become thoroughly tired of comic books and collecting. This is a mistake. If you sell under these conditions, you're much more likely to dump your collection for a lower price.

The typical collector often waits for one, two, three, or more years after he loses interest in comics before he finally decides to part with his comics. By this time, the market conditions have changed. He probably no longer knows which books are in demand and which titles are now selling well. Sell when it hurts. You'll be able to drive a harder bargain, and you won't accept the first offer that comes along.

Also, watch collecting trends. Sometimes it pays to hold onto a specific issue or title because collector interest may not have peaked yet. By waiting six months or a year, you could double or triple the price you get when you sell. On the other hand, there have been many comics that have suddenly lost their glamour.

Back in the 1970s there was a Marvel comic called *Howard the Duck*. Within three months after the first issue came out, it was selling for $3 —not a bad increase for a comic that originally cost 25 cents. Now let's follow that book through its ups and downs for the next several years.

Howard the Duck #1

Price Fluctuations for a Mint Copy

Date	Value (dollars)	Percentage Increase from Previous Year
January 1976	0.25	——
April 1976	3.00	+1,100
April 1977	7.50	+150
April 1978	12.00	+60
April 1979	15.00	+25
April 1980	12.00	−16
April 1981	10.00	−16
October 1982	8.00	−20
October 1983	7.00	−8
April 1984	7.00	−0
October 1984	6.00	−14

You can see from the chart that if you bought 100 copies of *Howard the Duck #1* off the newsstands in January 1976 for a total of $25 and then got full guide value for them in April 1979, you would have had a profit of $1,475! Not bad for a three-year investment.

On the other hand, suppose you bought 100 copies in April 1978 at $12 per copy. You saw the book go up in price the next year to $15. At this point, you could have sold all the books and made a $300 profit. But you decided to wait three more years before selling. After all, shouldn't the price go up still more? By that time, however, collectors had lost interest in the title, and the comic was worth $7—if you could find a buyer. From the $1,500 investment in 1978, you would now have only $700 worth of comics 36 months later. You would have lost $800.

The moral: Knowing when to sell is just as important as knowing which comics to buy. And if you wait until you feel like selling your collection, you may have waited too long—or perhaps not long enough.

Who Will Buy Your Comics?

Comics aren't like gold or stocks or bonds. You can't just take them anywhere and get money for them. And you're not going to be able to get immediate cash unless you find a ready buyer who wants every book you have. Selling comics is work. But the work is fun, and if you take your time and do it carefully, you'll be well rewarded.

There are two types of people who will buy your comics: dealers and collectors.

Selling to Dealers

A dealer wants to buy your comic books so that he can resell them for more money. From the profits he makes on selling your comics, he has to pay himself a salary, pay rent and other overhead, and pay for advertising, postage, insurance, and other expenses that arise from doing business.

Consequently, he wants to pay as little as possible for your comics so that he can make as much profit as possible. The difference between what he pays for a book and what he sells it for is called his *operating margin*. Typically, most retail stores operate on a 40–60-percent margin. That means that a dealer is going to be able to pay only around 50 percent of what he can sell a comic for.

You will more likely be offered 20–35 percent of what your collection is worth by the guide when you sell everything outright. On nice-condition books in high demand, you may get as much as 50–75 percent of the retail price.

The advantage in selling to a dealer is that he will usually buy all your comics—the good with the bad—and he will give you immediate cash.

Another advantage is that it's quick and easy to sell to a dealer, especially if he is in your town or within convenient driving distance.

You are also spared the trouble of having to individually grade and price each comic in your collection. An experienced dealer can often quote you an approximate price for all your comic books in just a few minutes.

Selling to a dealer is convenient and gets quick cash in your pocket. But you'll never get full value for your comics from a dealer. It's an economic fact of life.

Selling to Collectors

When you sell to another collector, you do two people a favor, yourself and the collector who buys your comics. Because you have no overhead and few expenses, unlike a professional dealer, you can sell your comics for less than what a dealer will charge. This helps out a fellow collector. On the other hand, you can still ask for more money for your books than a dealer will offer you.

For example, if a dealer sells a comic for $10, he may be able to offer you $3–5 for it. If you sell that same comic to a collector, you could ask $7 or $8 for it. You would make an extra $3 or $4, and the collector who buys the book from you would save a couple of bucks.

It sounds like the ideal way to sell your comics. And it is—if you're in no hurry and don't mind some extra work. Other collectors will rarely want all your comics. They may want only one or two particular issues to complete their own collections. This means that you have to offer your comics to many collectors before you'll be able to sell most of them. You might not be able to find a collector to buy some of your comics at any price.

To locate the right collector for your comics, you may have to spend money advertising. You may have to sell your books through the mail, which means packing and postage expenses.

Selling to other collectors, however, can be a lot of fun. You can make new friends and may be able to pick up other comics for your collection in trade. And you will make more money—eventually.

An ideal method is to sell to both collectors and dealers. Try to sell your more desirable comics to collectors on a book-by-book basis. Then, after a few more attempts, you can sell any remaining comics to a dealer at a bulk price.

The Different Ways of Selling Comics

Whether you sell to collectors or to dealers, you'll still have to find some way to get your comics to the marketplace. In the early days of comic collecting, almost all sales took place through the mail. There just

126

weren't any local comic shops or dealers or regional conventions where you could take your books to sell. Today you can still sell comic books by mail from the convenience of your home, or you can travel across town (or across the country!) to meet other collectors and dealers face to face.

Selling by Mail

You can sell your collection by mail to one of several hundred dealers across the country. Here's how to do it. First, get the names and addresses of several dealers who advertise in various collector publications and price guides as being in the market for comic books. Now sit down and list every comic book in your collection and its condition, like this:

Amazing Spider-Man	#13	Very Good
	#38	Fine
	#121	Good, small tear in cover
Avengers	#100	Near Mint

and so on.

Try to be as accurate as you can in your grading, but also remember that the dealer will double check and possibly regrade your collection when he receives it.

You do not need to list the value of the comic. In fact, you probably shouldn't put any prices at all on this list. Let the dealer make an offer; you just tell him what you have. For your own information, however, you should also look up the value of each comic in a price guide and figure up a rough estimate of what your collection would be worth by the guide.

Don't get excited and think that you will be offered anywhere near the full guide price, but do keep the total worth of your collection in mind. Some dealers may want to know what your collection "guides at," and if you can tell them, then they know that you have at least a general idea of your collection's value.

Now make several copies of your list; you don't want to lose it and have to do all that work again. Select at least three dealers and send them each a copy of your list, along with a self-addressed, stamped envelope for their reply. You may have to wait two or three weeks before you get an offer. If you are not offered at least 25 percent of what your collection is worth by the guide, try some other dealers. Remember that if you sell your collection by mail to a dealer, you'll have to pay the shipping costs.

If you accept an offer, wrap your books up well for shipping and always insure them for the full amount that the dealer offers you. Keep the dealer's offer letter in a safe place. You can use it to substantiate any insurance claims should the package get lost in the mail.

Almost all dealers will wait until they receive your comics and verify your grading before they will send you a check. This may take three days or three weeks, so wait at least that long before inquiring again.

Advertising Your Collection

Many collectors also sell by mail to other collectors. This is probably the best way to get the top price for your comics, and it is relatively cheap. Either you can advertise your comics in a display ad in one of the national collectors' newspapers or magazines, or you can simply make up your own list or catalog of comics that you have for sale and send it to interested collectors.

To make up a catalog of your comics, just use a list like the one you may have made to send to a dealer but include prices for each comic. Don't ask for offers; most collectors prefer to see the price you want.

List each comic separately with its grade and price. Describe any unusual defects in the comic and also indicate any special features or contents of the book, such as if a popular artist drew the comic or if the origin of a character is revealed in the book.

Your ad or sale list should include your address and telephone number. Many collectors like to call on the phone to reserve comics before they send their cash. Phone orders can help both you and the collector. You'll know ahead of time which comics will be sold, and the collector will be sure that he will be getting the comics that he is ordering.

You'll also need to have a paragraph or two in your ad or catalog that gives the collector ordering information and terms. In the ordering section, give the following information:

- How much extra money to include for postage and handling. When I first started collecting, dealers asked for 50–75 cents extra for packing and postage. Now the minimum amount requested is $1, and most of the time it's around $2–$3. Some dealers will pay the postage if the order is large enough.

- Whether a minimum order is required. Some people like to ask for a minimum order of $5, $10, or more. This way you won't spend all your time (and postage!) wrapping and sending very small orders. Asking for a minimum order may discourage some orders, however. A better way is to ask for a high enough postage-and-handling charge to cover your costs of processing small orders.

- How payment should be made. Most mail-order dealers prefer payment by money order or certified check. There is always the danger that a personal check may "bounce" and you'll lose the money. To prevent this, some advertisers specify in their ad or catalog that checks must clear the bank before the comics can be shipped. If you're going to hold someone's order until his check clears, be sure to specify that so he'll know the reason for any delay.

- Any returns policy. You should always give the buyer the option of returning a comic to you if he is not happy with the way you graded it. In your ad or list, state how quickly a comic must be returned to you for a refund. Generally, seven to ten days is long enough.

- Grading codes and condition standards. You may wish to list any grading abbreviations you use in your ad so that new collectors will understand it better. If you use different grading standards than are described in this book or *The Comic Book Price Guide,* then you should state what they are.

- Any trading information. Some collectors that advertise comics for sale or issue catalogs are also interested in trading comics for books they need for their own collections. If any of your advertised comics are available for trade, state which comics you are interested in trading for.

Selling by Auction

Another way to sell your comics by mail is through an auction. An auction is a good way to sell expensive and rare comics, as you might get a better offer than you would if you just advertised a scarce book at its guide price.

You can have an auction simply by listing your comics in a catalog or ad and then asking for bids, or offers, on each book. You should also have a cut-off date on which the auction will end, usually three to six weeks after you advertise.

Of course, you will always get some very low bids on some of your comics as people try to pick up bargains. You don't have to accept such low bids if you don't want to. In fact, you don't have to accept any offers that are made for your books if you are in charge of the auction.

There are professional auctioneers, however, that will take on your comics for their own auction lists. Usually, they'll charge about 10–20 percent of the price realized during the auction and send you the rest of the money. Before assigning your comics to another person for auction, be sure either that you have done business with him in the past or that he has excellent references.

Selling Comics at a Convention

Selling comics by mail is a leisurely process. It may take you several weeks or months to make up ads and catalogs, get orders, and mail the books out. At a comic book convention, the pace is fast and frantic. It's not unusual to sell $300 worth of comics in one hour, and you may deal with a new collector and buyer every two minutes. At the end of a convention day, you may come home hundreds or thousands of dollars richer (and also very, very tired!).

Actually, selling at a convention can be the best way for a collector to get top prices for his collection. Simply by setting up at a convention, you gain the status of a comic book dealer. You can now buy comics at dealer's prices at the convention, trade with other collectors, and charge retail prices.

The disadvantage is that there is a lot of competition at a convention. There will be dozens of other comic dealers and collectors who will be offering hundreds of thousands of comic books. Unless you have your comics at a very good price or unless they are extremely scarce, you'll get passed up by the collectors who are there looking for bargains.

To sell comics at a convention, you'll need to contact the organizers of the convention a few weeks or a few months before it takes place. You'll be able to rent a six- or eight-foot table to display your comics. If you have a lot of comics, you may want to rent two or three tables. A table at a convention costs anywhere from $20–150 to rent, depending on the size of the convention and how many days it runs. (Conventions generally last one to three days, although the major conventions run four days. Most conventions are two-day, weekend affairs.)

As soon as you rent your table, start preparing for the convention. First, you'll have to put each comic for sale in a plastic bag to protect it while at the convention. You'll also have to grade each book and determine how much you want for it, and then put a price sticker on the plastic bag.

Next you'll have to arrange your comics in storage boxes or notebooks. Most dealers at a convention put all their Marvel comics in one box, their DC comics in another box, and so on. They also arrange all the titles alphabetically within each box, and they may have dividers or place cards in the box that identify where each title starts and stops. They may also keep their more valuable books behind the table in a special display rack or in a locked briefcase. In addition, you may want to make up signs for your table and boxes of comics that identify them and also indicate any special prices, discounts, or highly sought-after books. If this sounds like a lot of work, it is!

You should start preparing for a convention at least one or two weeks before you go. It takes more time than you can imagine to price every comic you have for sale. But do make sure that you put a price on each comic! Nothing is so frustrating to a collector as to pick up an unpriced comic and have to ask how much the seller wants for it. Most people won't waste the time or make the effort to ask you the price of a comic. At every convention, you'll always see some collector or dealer who is desperately trying to price and sell his comics at the same time. Price your comics before you go to the convention. You'll sell a lot more.

And when you price your comics, keep in mind that there will be many other collectors and dealers at the convention who will be selling the same comic books as you. Try to give your customers a bargain so that they will buy from you. Ask yourself as you price each comic how much you would be willing to pay for it. When in doubt, set a lower price on it. Even by asking low prices, you'll probably still end up going home with most of the comics that you took to the convention.

You'll sell a lot of comics, too. Don't be afraid to wheel and deal at the convention. If other collectors are interested in buying several comics from you, give them discounts or toss in free comics. You'll find that they will tell their friends or return to your table themselves for more good deals. Take time to talk to the collectors. Ask them what comics they collect and which ones they are looking for. Be helpful and show them some books that they might be interested in. Talk to them about your own collecting interests. Conventions are social occasions, and people come there to have a good time as well as to do business. If you're friendly, cheerful, and outgoing, you'll sell more comics from your own table.

When you have a table at a convention, be sure that you get there as early as possible. At most conventions, the dealers are allowed to set up their tables at least one hour before the show starts. During this set-up hour, you have time to carefully arrange your comics, make sure they are all priced, and visit with the other dealers at the show. Many times the best deals of the convention are made during the "dealer's hour" before the show actually starts. Other dealers will come to your table looking for merchandise that they can buy and then resell later. When dealers sell to each other at a convention, it is customary to offer some sort of dealer discount.

If you can find anyone to accompany you to a convention, grab him— friend, foe, spouse, child, or parent. You really need two people to sell comics at a convention. Quite often you will need to get a bite to eat, go to the rest room, or leave your table to make other good deals. Someone should remain at the table at all times to watch over your comics and to make sales.

At some point, you may even need two people to take the money in! During the first two hours of a convention, especially, cash flies fast and furious. You may need more than two hands just to count out change (a pleasant thought, no doubt). And during the slow periods, a partner at your table gives you someone to talk to and enjoy the convention with.

Selling at a Retail Store

Besides selling through the mail and at conventions, the other common way of getting money for your collection is to take it to a retail comic book dealer. These dealers may also be found at conventions or flea markets, or they may have a retail comic book shop.

Before you box up your comics and take them to a retail dealer, you should first call and make sure that he has the time and interest to see you. Sometimes a dealer may not be buying any comics at all, or it might be a very busy retail day (such as Saturday) that will prevent him from giving full attention to your books.

When you take your comics to a dealer, it's a good idea to separate your most valuable comics from the rest of the collection. A few good books can get lost in the huge pile of common comics and may be overlooked or discounted by a dealer. Arrange your comics by title and number. Make your books look like a carefully cared-for collection and not just some hodge-podge of extra comics that you had lying around. Also make sure that your valuable comics are protected in bags. Remove any old price stickers from the bags, and replace the bag itself if it is old and worn.

A dealer may ask you outright how much you want for your comics. Be careful. Too low a price and you lose money; too high and the dealer will lose interest. It's usually best to say nothing about what you expect to get. If a dealer keeps asking you what you want for the books, you can tell him about how much the comics are worth by the guide, and then ask for his offer. If he offers only 20–30 percent of the guide value, you can ask for up to 40 percent, or even 60 percent if the books are in demand. If you're selling fairly common comics, you should try to get at least 25 percent of the price-guide value. Let the dealer know you're willing to negotiate, however, and don't make take-it-or-leave-it offers.

If you are truly unhappy with the dealer's offer, do not make any unpleasant remarks such as "You jerk! What are you trying to do, steal them from me?" Instead, take your books to another dealer, or hold onto them and hope you may be offered more for them later. You can always try the same dealer later (if you don't insult him) or offer him a selected portion of your collection.

When a dealer is examining your books, he may simply flip through them very quickly and then quote you a price without even looking up any of the comics in a guide. This is normal. Most dealers already know about what the comic is selling for, whether they need it, and how much they can ask for it when they offer it for sale. Quite often an experienced

132

dealer can look through a thousand-book collection and give you an accurate price for it within 30 minutes.

If you don't like the price offered you for an especially rare and valuable comic, you can always ask the dealer whether he will try to sell the book for you on consignment. This means that the dealer does not pay you for the comic until he sells it. If he does sell it, he will usually keep about 20–35 percent of the money for himself as his commission and give you the rest. Actually, you can sometimes make more money by having a comic sold on consignment. Of course, you have to wait until it does sell, and if it doesn't, you have to take the comic back.

Sometimes consignment is the only way that a dealer will handle an extremely expensive comic book worth several hundred dollars. He may not want to tie up his money in a high-priced book that may take months to sell. And you may also be able to realize a larger profit on a comic sold on consignment. Either way, it's worth a try.

All too often, collectors neglect the selling side of comic collecting. After all, for most people it's a lot more fun to buy and read comics than it is to get rid of them. Yet selling is the other half of collecting, and the sooner you learn how to trade your books for bucks, the better off you'll be when it comes time to buy more.

After all, the smartest comic book buyer is the person who knows that he must sell them eventually as well.

QUESTIONS ABOUT COMIC BOOKS AND COLLECTING

Who has the biggest collection of comics? And how many comics does the average collector own?

The Library of Congress collection of comics numbers about 45,000 different books. This is the largest public comic book collection. There are some private collectors with nearly that many books, but exact figures are difficult to verify because collectors with extremely large collections usually like to remain anonymous due to fears about thefts.

The typical comic collector has a collection of 500–5,000 comic books. Some of the bigger comic book dealers may have stocks of 200,000 to 1 million books, but of course many of these issues are duplicates of popular titles.

Some of the largest known comic collections number from 25,000 to 50,000 *different* issues. To give you an idea of the size of such collections, here's the comic collector's yardstick: Ten stacked comic books equal one inch. By measuring the stacks of your collection in inches and then multiplying by ten, you can get an approximation of how many comics you own.

If you're one of the big-time collectors that has around 35,000 comic books, that translates to about 100 yards of comics stacked back to back. Touchdown!

How long will a comic book last until it falls apart?

Of course, this answer depends on how you store the comic and what protective measures you take. A typical comic book, stored under *average* conditions, will last for about 40 to 50 years. If you store the comic book in a cool, dry, dark location, however, it will last for 75 to 80 years before it starts to crumble.

On the other hand, a comic that is in a hot, humid environment without any protection will deteriorate rapidly after only 12–15 years.

Simply by storing your comic in an acid-free environment and using

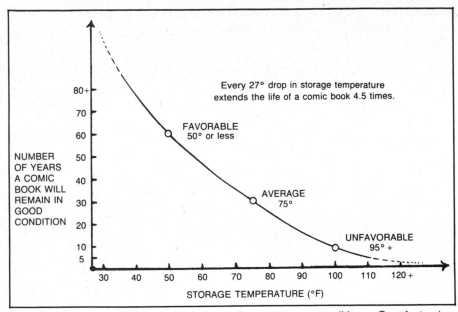

How long a comic book will last depends on storage conditions. One factor is temperature; the cooler you keep your comics, the longer they will remain in good condition.

Mylar bags, you can extend your comic's life to 125 years or more. A chemically deacidified book may remain intact for 150–200 years. If you're still reading comic books by then, you'll probably require some preservation yourself.

I've noticed that on comic books published after 1980 there is a small box in the lower left-hand corner of the cover. Sometimes this box is full of lines, and on other comics the box may give some sort of picture or company emblem. What is that box on the cover all about?

Congratulations. You've just located the UPC box. UPC stands for "Universal Product Code," and it is placed on comics to help the distributor keep track of which comics are returned by retailers. Here's how it works:

When comic books are unsold on the newsstands, they are shipped back to the comic book distributor. The distributor uses an optical-scanning device to read the UPC box on the cover. This box has what is known as a *bar code,* which is the same sort of code that you can find on a can of soup or almost any other retail product. Those little lines inside the box identify each comic by title, publisher, price, etc. As the comic books are returned, the bar codes are electronically read and the proper publisher is charged for the unsold books that are shipped back.

Now you may have noticed that sometimes instead of identification lines filling up the UPC box on the cover, there may be instead a picture of Spider-Man if it's a Marvel comic, or perhaps just a company's name, such as "DC Comics," inside the UPC box. This is done to identify comics that are sold by the publisher on a nonreturnable basis. Since these comics cannot be returned to the distributor if they do not sell, there is no reason to have a bar code box on the cover to identify the comic.

Most comic book stores buy their comics on a nonreturnable basis because (1) it's cheaper for them to buy the books that way and (2) they usually keep any unsold new comics for back-issue stock anyway. On the other hand, regular newsstands and traditional retailers buy their comics on a returnable basis because they want the distributor to take back any unsold comics at the end of each month.

From the comic book publisher's viewpoint, there are two types of comics: returnable and nonreturnable. Returnable comics have a bar code in the UPC box on the cover, while nonreturnable comics have a standarized company emblem in the cover box. Other than the differences in the UPC box on the cover, returnable and nonreturnable comics are identical.

My advice: Read the comic and forget about the little boxes. Life is too short.

What is the most valuable comic in the world? What is the rarest?

For many years, the most valuable comic has been *Action Comics #1,* which introduced Superman to the world. Within the last several years, however, *Marvel Comics #1,* which introduced many of the popular Golden Age Marvel heroes has been the most expensive comic book. Due to the historical significance of both *Action Comics #1* and *Marvel Comics #1,* it's safe to say that one of these two books will probably always be the most valuable comic in the world.

These two, however, are not the rarest comic books in the world. There are several copies of both *Action Comics #1* and *Marvel Comics #1*—in fact, there are probably more existing copies of *Action #1* than there are for *Action #2* or *#3.*

There are several "rarest" comics in the world, because there are several dozen comics of which there is only one known copy. You can't get much rarer than only one existing issue!

Some of the really rare books may exist only in publishers' and artists' files and may not even be available on the collector's market. In the last few years, several such comics have turned up, such as *Tab, the Comic Weekly* in the private files of the artist Will Eisner and a copy of *Whiz*

Comics #1 (originally entitled *Flash Comics #1*) in the files of a defunct publisher.

So there are several "rarest" comic books, but only one most valuable comic. And the most valuable comic is always the one that has sold most recently for the highest price.

How are the prices determined in a comic book price guide? What do these prices really mean?

Prices in a guide for any type of collectible (coins, stamps, comics, antiques, or whatever) are only estimates. These estimated prices are derived from recorded sales of certain rare items, dealer's price lists, and market information as supplied by both the buyer and seller.

In some cases, the prices represent educated guesses and simply arbitrary decisions based on a person's long-standing knowledge of the comic book field. It is impossible to gather price data for every comic book in existence. For one thing, not all comic books even come up for sale in a year's time. In these cases, the prices usually reflect the overall comic book market.

For example, suppose a copy of *Captain America Comics* from 1942 was worth about $400 in 1984. Maybe that particular issue of *Captain America* was not even sold that year, but if similar comics from that year and publisher had increased 25 percent in value, then it might be reasonable to assume that this particular issue of *Captain America* was also worth 25 percent more, which would put its new value at $500.

For the more recent and widely sold comics, such as the newer Marvel and DC titles; there is a large base of information to draw upon to determine the average selling prices. These comics are advertised on many lists, they are sold at most conventions, and there is common knowledge as to how much they are worth and whether they are increasing in value.

A price guide is simply an estimate, an approximation, a good guess as to the current value of a comic. It is not absolute fact. Remember that price guides are just that—they are *guides* to prices. Use them to guide yourself in your purchases and sales, but don't rely on them blindly.

Which comics are the best investments?

The comic books that have made the most money for their owners are usually those that were purchased in the medium price range for back-issue comics. The medium range, in this case, means comics that are worth $10–100.

Comics that cost more than $100 generally appreciate at a slower rate since there is limited collector demand for a comic as it becomes more and more expensive. On the other hand, inexpensive comics in the $2–

10 price range may not have the investment appeal that will cause their prices to increase.

Comics that cost $10–100 are usually on their way up. They are no longer considered cheap, but neither are they approaching their full potential, as the more expensive books have done. In other words, medium-priced comics have room to grow.

Many collectors spend a good portion of their back-issue money on comics that are under $100. They want to buy these moderately priced books before they increase too rapidly in value. As a result, there is a lot of interest and activity in the medium-range comics, and the wise investor can select those books that show a good potential for growth.

Should I insure my comic collection?

If you have a substantial amount of money invested in a few select comics, then insurance is a necessity. On the other hand, if you own several hundred or thousand comics that are worth only $1–3 each, it may not be very practical to insure them.

Most insurance companies will want some sort of inventory list or record of your collection, along with an estimated worth of the books. If you've already drawn up a have list for your collection, with the books' conditions and prices listed, then it's an easy step to getting them insured.

If you already have a homeowner's insurance policy, your collection may be covered automatically. Still, to substantiate any claims, you're going to have to have some sort of record of the comics you own. Since collectors generally buy and sell comics continuously, it's hard to keep a complete and current inventory. For this reason, large collections of low-value books may be more trouble to insure than they are worth.

On the other hand, if you own several comics that are worth $100 or more, insurance against theft and damage may ease your mind. One good solution to the insurance problem for very expensive comics is simply to rent a bank safety-deposit box. You can store from 10 to 50 comics or more depending on the size of the box, and you know that your irreplaceable books are well protected.

It seems that old comic books can cost a lot of money. How about some ways to get more comics for less money if you're collecting on a budget?

You don't have to spend a lot of money to assemble a really nice comic collection. Over 80 percent of all comics published in the last 15 years can be purchased for $1 or less. Some collectors refuse to spend more than $5 or $10 for any comic book, yet they own thousands of comics from the 1940s to the present day, including some rare and #1 comics issues.

Although certain comics can be expensive, you can build a collection on a limited budget that will still give you hours of enjoyment. You just have to know a few tricks that will stretch your comic dollar.

Cheap Trick #1: Reprints!

Reprints are the answer for the financially strapped comic collector. For a fraction of the cost of an expensive back issue, you can read stories you'd never see otherwise. Fortunately, Marvel and DC Comics have been generous in reprinting popular titles. It is possible, for example, to collect the first 150 issues or so of Spider-Man comics in reprinted form for under $100 total. You could spend ten times that much just for the first two original issues.

Many Golden Age comics from the 1940s have been reprinted in annuals and special giant-size issues since the late 1960s, and what's even better is that these reprint comics, annuals, and one-shot reprints still sell for very low prices as back issues.

Not only have comic book publishers reprinted some of their more popular titles and stories, but other book publishers have collected and reprinted comic strips, comic stories, and even the entire output of a particular comic book artist or company. Some of these reprints are printed on much-higher-quality paper than the originals so that they will last longer and remain in better condition. Occasionally (although not often enough), the reprinted comics will even be reproduced better than the originals, with better clarity and color quality.

The drawback to collecting reprints is that they will never be worth as much as the originals, and you may have a hard time selling them when you dispose of your collection. Of course, since you don't have a lot of money tied up in the reprinted issues, it's not so important that you regain your investment anyway. Besides, the pleasure of just reading the stories may be enough to justify the cost of a reprinted comic.

Reprints serve another valuable role as well. Many collectors will buy reprinted versions of rare comics that they have in their own collections. They read the reprint version and keep the more expensive original comic stored safely away from greasy fingers, spilled drinks, and nuclear attacks.

Cheap Trick #2: Naked Comics

Have you ever seen an undressed comic? Well-loved and well-read comics often lose their covers over years of reading and rereading. Coverless comics are rarely sought after by collectors; they prefer their comics well dressed, covered up, and complete.

In fact, coverless comics are so disdained by collectors, who want their books in top condition, that the prices for them are incredibly low. I've purchased comics that would normally sell for $50–100 for only 50 cents or a dollar simply because the cover was missing.

It's true that a comic's cover is sometimes the best part of the comic, but at savings of 100–1,000 percent, the collector on a budget cannot afford to ignore coverless comics.

Of course, you don't want to buy cheap or common or recent comics that are coverless, unless you simply want a reading copy that you don't have to worry about damaging. One collecting friend has a stack of coverless comics from the mid-1960s that he reads while soaking in the bathtub. If he drops one in the tub, the worst that will happen is that he'll lose a 25-cent investment and maybe turn four different colors from the running inks.

But the real savings in buying coverless comics comes from those books that are routinely priced in the $10–100 price range when in complete condition. You should look for coverless books that still have relatively white pages, are not brittle, and have no other pages missing. A nice, tight copy of a coverless comic will even last longer than a heavily browning comic with a cover.

With the ever-accelerating prices for old and rare comics, coverless comics are one of the real bargains left.

Cheap Trick #3: Be Unpopular

It's no secret that only a small percentage of all the comic titles ever published are prime collector's items. The truth is that the great majority of comics are rarely sought after or even collected by most people. So what does this mean? Well, if you don't mind being "unpopular," you can save a lot of money.

By concentrating on titles that are not in high demand by other collectors, you can assemble an interesting and unique collection at low cost. For example, almost everybody collects one or more Marvel hero titles, and as a result early issues of such comics can become very expensive. But there are only a few collectors who specialize in collecting Marvel *western* comics, and even far fewer that collect Marvel romance comics from the 1960s, to give just two examples.

At any one time, there is strong collector interest in probably fewer than two or three hundred comic titles—past and present. That leaves over 17,000 other comic titles that are not in high demand. By collecting unpopular titles, you are in an excellent position to bargain and buy at substantial discounts. I've gotten many comics that were highly enjoyable to read and fun to collect for about one-fourth of their true market value. On the other hand, I've seen collectors pay twice what a popular comic is really worth just because the competition was so fierce.

The point is that there are so many comics to collect, why follow the crowd and collect the same titles that everybody else is after? Remember that unpopularity does not mean that the comics are no good or poorly drawn or badly written; it may mean only that they haven't yet been discovered by collectors.

Since mint-condition comic books are the most valuable, should I buy only Mint comics for my collection?

If you are collecting comics that were published in the last ten to fifteen years, it's not that difficult or expensive to buy only Mint-condition books. Most dealers and collectors want their recent comics to be in Near-Mint or Mint condition, and you would have a hard time selling newer comics that are only in Good or Very Good condition.

If you insist on only Mint comics for your older issues, however, you're going to become frustrated and broke. For one thing, comics more than 20 years old are very difficult to locate in Mint condition. And since they usually cost five to seven times as much as the same comics in a lesser condition, your collection will be all that much more limited.

Don't become a slave to condition or a "Mint nut." There are some excellent comics to be enjoyed and collected that will probably be available only in fine or less condition. Many longtime collectors have decided that it's more important to them to have a large and wide-ranging collection of comics in only Very Good or Good condition than it is to have a small accumulation of Mint-perfect books.

My advice is to select a few titles or types of comics that you want to collect only in Mint or Near-Mint condition. Then set aside another portion of your collection that will allow for books in Fine or less condition. For example, I have a collection of comics from the 1940s that are all in at least Very Good condition. My comics from the early 1960s are in at least Fine condition, and any comics published after that, I try to get in only Near-Mint or Mint contition.

The point is that you alone should decide which condition you can live with. A very few collectors will not have any comic in their collection that is not absolutely perfect, and there are other collectors who don't care at all what shape the comic is in, just so they can read it.

The exception to this rule is that comic books that are purchased for investment and that cost a substantial amount of money should probably be in Fine or better condition. High-priced comics in the lower grades (Very Good, Good, Fair) are often difficult to sell and do not increase in value as quickly as investment-grade books.

Why do new comics have a date on them that is three or four months ahead of the date they're actually issued?

141

This practice of postdating comics began in the 1930s so that a comic could stay on the newsstand for a longer length of time. For example, if a comic came out in April but had a July date on its cover, then the newsstand dealer would be more likely to let the comic stay on sale until its cover date (some three or four months later) before he decided to return it to the publisher.

All through this book, you've barely mentioned the oldest tradition of all in comic collecting—trading comic books! How about some equal time for us collectors who would rather trade than buy or sell?

I've been saving the best for last. Comic collecting had its beginnings in the trading sessions of long ago. Collectors and readers with copies of comics they no longer wanted would get together with other comic fans and exchange issue for issue. There was no thought about the price of a comic. The books were traded and passed around for the pure enjoyment of having something new to read at no additional expense.

Collectors still trade comics, although now they are much more likely to do it "by the book." The book in this case is usually a standard price guide so that both collectors receive an equal cash value of comics in trade. If you have a comic that I want, I would offer you comics of equal value in exchange, according to a standard price guide. In this way, there is little room for disagreement over who got the better deal.

Of course, there are times when a collector will offer more than equal value for a book that he particularly wants. He may have many copies of relatively cheap and common comics that he wants to trade for one rare and valuable comic. In such a case, he may offer two or three or four times the value of the comic in trade, just to get the book he wants and to get rid of comics he no longer needs.

Although collectors do tend to trade by the book, all is fair in love, war, and comic book exchanges. The only rule is that both people who trade must be completely satisfied with the deal. If either person decides that the trade is unfair, due to misgrading or misunderstanding, then all books should be returned with no questions asked.

Trading is a great way to get new comics and to unload ones you no longer want. And it is not unfair to drive a hard bargain. If you have a book that some other collector wants very badly, then make him offer you a very good trade for it. On the other hand, if you want a particular item from another collector's personal collection, then you had better be prepared to make an outstanding offer for the book.

Trading is a one-on-one proposition and can make you a sharper and more astute collector. Just remember: It's not a good trade unless both people are happy.

After all, we are doing this for fun now, aren't we?

THE FUTURE OF
COMIC COLLECTING

For a relatively young hobby, comic collecting has a bright future. Every year, new comic readers and fans are discovering the joys of collecting their favorite comic titles. The circulations of collector's publications, price guides, comic indexes, and other comic-related books are soaring. More and more old comic books and comic strips are being collected and reissued in hardbound editions for future generations to enjoy.

A comic collection, carefully chosen and cared for, will almost certainly appreciate in value and yield a good return on an enjoyable investment.

The past and present state of comic collecting indicates that the future will be even brighter. What is coming up ahead in the next decade of this hobby?

The Computers Are Coming!

Perhaps one of the greatest impacts on the comic-collecting field will come in the form of personal computers and computer networks. Already many collectors, dealers, and investors in the stamp- and coin-collecting fields are using computers and computer networks to keep abreast of their hobby. The computerization of the comic field is fast approaching.

The day will come when both comic collectors and dealers will meet, not through the mail or at conventions, but over computer networks. Comics will be bought, sold, and traded via computer communications. Price updates will occur almost daily instead of annually. A collector will be able to find the current price and availability of almost any comic in the world via a computer terminal.

The Comic Book Price Guide itself, or one similar to it, will probably also be available in a computerized format. Collectors will be able to access a comprehensive comic book data base on a home computer and retrieve all types of information about their favorite comic books and artists. Collectors will also communicate over their computer lines, and information will be quickly exchanged and built upon.

The Collector's Market Will Grow

During the last five years, the specialized collector's marketplace for new comics has increased tremendously—almost to the point where it dominates and shapes the current trends of new comic books.

Comic book publishers will continue to cater to this specialized market, while at the same time providing more and varied comics to the general comic-reading population. Special editions, limited series, and comics printed on high-quality paper will increase in numbers in an effort to appeal to the built-in comic-collecting marketplace.

Independent comic book publishers will continue to thrive as they find their niche among the traditional and mainstream comic publishers. Many more comics will be produced that aim at a wider audience, and comics will play an increasing role in education and literacy projects.

Collecting Trends

For the next several years, collectors will continue to concentrate on new comic releases. Back-issue comics will still be in demand, but much of the speculation will focus on the new comic titles.

Investors will be buying more carefully and choosing truly scarce comics in top condition. As a result, there may be real bargains to be had in the low-to-medium-price back-issue comics, especially those from the late 1940s through the early 1960s. As investors concentrate more and more on Mint-condition comics, collectors will find the lower-price Fine and Good comics to be good buys.

Comics from the years 1965 through 1980 will continue to be in very plentiful supply, as collections assembled during these years are liquidated by collectors leaving the hobby.

There will continue to be interest in reprinting classic comics in an effort to preserve them beyond their normal readership span. Look for an inexpensive method, perhaps video in nature, that will allow comics to be conveniently stored in another media and then recalled by collectors and researchers. The technology now exists that would allow every comic book in the Library of Congress to be recorded on a single video disk and to be viewed by a collector in his own home!

Comics themselves are too fragile to be maintained for more than 40 or 50 years, so there will be new research in storing comic books on more permanent media. In addition, there may be a real breakthrough in comic book and paper preservation in the next ten years that will allow economical and wide-scale preservation of older comics.

Predictions and speculation are always risky, and the comic-collecting marketplace always holds surprises for seers and prophets. But there is one thing that you can be certain of: The most exciting hobby today and tomorrow is comic book collecting! You're going to have a lot of fun.

APPENDIX: HOW TO BECOME AN EXPERT: SOURCE MATERIALS FOR THE COLLECTOR

No single book can tell you everything there is to know about collecting comic books or the comics themselves.

Each month, hundreds of pages are written about comics and collecting in various fan magazines, newspapers, and collector publications. More new books with comic book and comic strip reprints are being published in larger quantities and wider circulations than ever before. Clearly there is an explosion of information about comics, and the collector must do his best to keep up with the field.

This appendix can get you started in your quest to learn more about collecting comics. Information and addresses in this appendix will become more quickly dated than the rest of the book, so always write for current details about the books, magazines, and organizations described here.

Collector and Fan Publications

The following magazines, newspapers, and books are excellent sources of material for the serious comic fan and collector:

The Comics Buyer's Guide
Krause Publications
700 E. State St.
Iola, WI 54990

The Comics Buyer's Guide has been published, in one format or another, since 1971. It's primarily an ad magazine and newspaper for collectors, and each issue features thousands of old comic books for sale as well as news about the current comic scene.

Published weekly, it's fandom's meeting place and the closest thing that comic fans and the comic industry have to an "official" voice. Absolutely essential for anyone interested in buying and selling comics. Free sample copy upon request.

The Comic Reader
Street Enterprises
P.O. Box 255
Menominee Falls, WI 53051

The Comic Reader is one of the oldest continually published fanzines. In fact, this author was first introduced to the world of fandom within its pages in the early 1960s.

The magazine concentrates on news about current comics and their creators. It also has a number of regular opinion columns and an interesting letter page. Some comic strips are reprinted, and it has a pleasant, informative style that will entertain both the casual and the experienced comic fan and collector. Send a self-addressed, stamped envelope for current subscription rates.

The Comics Journal
Fantagraphics
196 W. Haviland La.
Stamford, CT 06903

The Comics Journal is a large, slick magazine that is packed with comic news, comic book reviews, a long letter column, and in-depth interviews with comic book artists, writers, and editors.

The emphasis is usually on the current comic scene, and the writers for the magazine are known for their forthright opinions and analyses. Send a self-addressed, stamped envelope for current subscription rates.

There are dozens of other excellent collector magazines and newspapers. Unfortunately, many appear and disappear in the span of a single year, so it is hard to keep up with them. To help you locate other collector publications, you may want to order:

Fandom Directory
Fandom Computer Services
P.O. Box 4278
San Bernardino, CA 92409

The Fandom Directory lists most of the major conventions, fan clubs, fan magazines, and events for each year. In addition, it contains the names and addresses of over 10,000 comic fans and collectors, listed by state.

The directory is published every year and is an invaluable source book for the comic fan and collector. You can use this directory to locate nearby comic stores, to order current issues of fan publications, and to find out about upcoming conventions and club meetings. Send a self-addressed, stamped envelope for the price of the current directory.

Collector's Price Guides

The most commonly used comic book price guide is The Comic Book Price Guide, edited by Robert M. Overstreet. There are other price guides published, and these may be consulted for additional information and comparison.

Almost all comic book dealers, however, use the Overstreet price guide in their transactions. Most collectors also seem to prefer the Overstreet guide to all others and generally buy, sell, and trade comics based at least in part on the prices in this guide.

A price guide is the most essential reference work a collector can buy. Not only will a good guide help you figure approximately what your comics are worth, but it can also tell you how many issues of a comic were published, who drew the comic, and many other facts about a comic that would be of interest to a collector.

Since the Overstreet guide does not list underground comics, there is also a price guide just for these books. You should be able to find both price guides in most major bookstores. If not, here are the addresses where you can obtain these two publications:

The Comic Book Price Guide, Robert M. Overstreet, editor. Distributed by Harmony Books, Crown Publishers, One Park Ave., New York, NY 10016. New edition each year.

Overstreet Publications, Inc.
780 Hunt Cliff Dr. N.W.
Cleveland, TN 37311

The Official Underground and Newave Comix Price Guide, by Jay Kennedy. Distributed by Harmony Books, Crown Publishers, One Park Ave., New York, NY 10016, 1982.

Boatner Norton Press
99 Mt. Auburn St.
Cambridge, MA 02138

Library Books and Other Reference Works

The following books may be found in public libraries, or can be ordered from the publisher if they're still in print:

Aldridge, Alan, and George Perry, The Penguin Book of Comics (Harmondsworth, Eng.: Penguin Books, 1967).

Bails, Jerry, and Hames Ware, eds., The Who's Who of American Comic Books (4 vols.), 1973–1976 (Jerry Bails, 21101 E. 11 Mile, Saint Clair Shores, MI 48081).

Barrier, Michael and Martin Williams, eds., A Smithsonian Book of Comic-Book Comics (New York: Smithsonian Institution Press, 1981).

Blackbeard, Bill, and Martin Williams, eds., The Smithsonian Collection of Newspaper Comics (New York: Smithsonian Institution Press, 1977).

Daniels, Les, Comix: A History of Comic Books in America (New York: Outerbridge and Dienstfrey, 1971).

Estren, Mark, A History of Underground Comics (San Francisco: Straight Arrow Books, 1974).

Feiffer, Jules, The Great Comic Book Heroes (New York: Dial Press, 1965).

Goulart, Ron, The Adventurous Decade (New Rochelle, NY: Arlington House, 1975).

Hirsh, Michael and Patrick Lambert, The Great Canadian Comic Books (Toronto: Peter Martin, 1971).

Horn, Maurice, ed., World Encyclopedia of Comics (New York: Avon, 1977).

Lupoff, Richard, and Donald Thompson, eds., All in Color for a Dime (New Rochelle, NY: Arlington House, 1970).

Steranko, James, ed., The Steranko History of Comics (2 vols.) (Reading, PA: Supergraphics, 1970 and 1972).

Thompson, Donald, and Richard Lupoff, eds., The Comic-Book Book (New Rochelle, NY: Arlington House, 1973).

Wertham, Frederic, Seduction of the Innocent (New York: Rinehart and Co., 1954).

Libraries and Museums

Imagine going to a library and being able to read hundreds of old comic books from the 1940s to the present! You can do just that if you live near some of the libraries and museums listed below.

These libraries maintain special collections of comic books for research purposes. They will also accept donated collections of comic books, so if you ever want to give your comics a good home where they will be appreciated and taken care of, then consider contacting some of these libraries. Michigan State University in particular has facilities for donated collections.

If you plan to visit these libraries to look at their comic collections, contact the director of special collections first. Often you must have permission and an appointment to view these rare comics and original comic art.

Libraries with Special Comic Collections

University of California at Berkeley, Berkeley, CA
California State University, Fullerton, CA
University of California at Los Angeles, Los Angeles, CA
Library of Congress, Washington, DC
University of Chicago, Chicago, IL
Southern Illinois University, Edwardsville, IL
Indiana University, Bloomington, IN
Iowa State University, Ames, IA
University of Maryland, Catonsville, MD
Michigan State University, East Lansing, MI
Fairleigh Dickinson University, Rutherford, NJ
Bowling Green State University, Bowling Green, OH
Ohio State University, Columbus, OH
University of Oregon, Eugene, OR
University of Pittsburgh, Pittsburgh, PA
College de Sherbrooke, Sherbrooke, Quebec, Canada

Museums with Comic Books and Original Comic Art

San Francisco Academy of Comic Art, San Francisco, CA
Comics Magazine Association of America, New York, NY
Museum of Comic Art, Port Chester, NY

ABOUT THE AUTHOR

Mike Benton has been a comic book collector, dealer, and investor for the last 20 years.

He has written on comics and collecting for such publications as *The Comics Collector, The Comics Buyer's Guide, Comic Scene Magazine, Collectibles Illustrated,* and *The American Collector.*

Besides being a collector and fan, Mike has operated a mail-order comic book business for 15 years and has organized and produced comic book conventions.

He also is a technical writing consultant for the computer industry and has written computer manuals and documentation for several worldwide corporations. He is the author of the book *The Complete Guide to Computer Camps and Workshops.*